CONTENTS

FROM RUSSIA WITH LOVE

COSTUMES FOR THE BALLETS RUSSES 1909–1933

 ■ national gallery of **australia**

Edited designed and produced by the Publications Department of the National Gallery of Australia, Canberra.

Designed by Kirsty Morrison
Edited by Susan Hall
Colour separations by ColourboxDigital
Printed by Lamb Printers

CONTRIBUTORS

Roger Leong is Assistant Curator, International Decorative Arts, National Gallery of Australia, Canberra.

Natalia Metelitsa is Deputy Director, Head of Research and International Relations at the St Petersburg State Museum of Theatre and Music, St Petersburg.

Nancy Van Norman Baer was Curator, Theater and Dance Collection, Fine Arts Museums of San Francisco.

Lynn Garafola is a freelance dance critic and historian living in New York.

Sarah Woodcock is Research Assistant at the Theatre Museum of the Victoria and Albert Museum, London.

Michelle Potter is Manager of the *Keep Dancing* project, National Film and Sound Archive, Canberra.

Cataloguing-in-Publication-data

From Russia with love: costumes for the Ballets russes 1909–1933

ISBN 0 642 54116 7

1. Diaghilev, Serge, 1872–1929 - Exhibitions. 2. Ballets russes - Exhibitions. 3. Ballet - Costume - Exhibitions. 4. Ballet - Stage-setting and scenery - Exhibitions. I. Leong, Roger, 1961 –. II. National Gallery of Australia.

792.80940749471

(front cover) **Alexandre Benois** Costume for a musician in *Le Pavillon d'Armide* (detail) National Gallery of Australia, Canberra © Alexandre Benois, 1909/ADAGP, Reproduced by permission of VISCOPY Ltd, Sydney
(back cover) **Michel Larionov** Costume design for the Chief Clown in *Chout* Victoria and Albert Museum, London © Michel Larionov, 1915/ADAGP. Reproduced by permission of VISCOPY Ltd, Sydney
(frontispiece) **Count Jean de Strelecki** *Portrait of Serge Diaghilev* St Petersburg State Museum of Theatre and Music

This publication accompanies the exhibition *From Russia with Love: Costumes for the Ballets Russes 1909–1933* organised by the National Gallery of Australia and curated by Roger Leong and Christine Dixon, National Gallery of Australia.

Art Gallery of Western Australia, Perth
6 February–5 April 1999

National Gallery of Australia, Canberra
15 May–1 August 1999

LENDERS TO THE EXHIBITION

The Australian Ballet, Melbourne

A.A. Bakhrushin State Central Theatre Museum, Moscow

Comité André Masson, Paris

Musée national d'art moderne—Centre de création industrielle, Centre Georges Pompidou, Paris

National Film and Sound Archive, Canberra

Österreichisches Theatermuseum, Vienna

St Petersburg State Museum of Theatre and Music

Theatre Museum, Victoria and Albert Museum, London

Victoria and Albert Museum, London

FOREWORD

The performances of the Ballets Russes of Serge Diaghilev were by all accounts magnificent. *From Russia with Love: Costumes for the Ballets Russes 1909–1933* traces the story of the Ballets Russes through the work of the company's designers — the costumes, the original drawings and the sets. With the inclusion of music, film and photographs, this exhibition is designed to evoke the magical sights, sounds and sense of a Ballets Russes performance.

Many of the works illustrated in this book, which accompanies the exhibition, are from the collection of the National Gallery of Australia, for which much credit is owed to founding director, James Mollison. Complementing the National Gallery's extensive holdings of Ballets Russes material are costumes, and particularly drawings, on loan from museums and collections in Russia, France, England and Austria, making this the most comprehensive survey of the Ballets Russes ever seen in Australia.

The enthusiasm and commitment to the exhibition given by the St Petersburg State Museum of Theatre and Music has been decisive. We thank the Director, Irina Evstigneeva. We are also indebted to the Deputy Director, Natalia Metelitsa, for her key personal role in the exhibition. They understand so well how ballet can be a social occasion, a family event for young and old, a celebration of movement, courage, design and beauty, and a profound aesthetic experience.

This project has involved many years of dedicated work. Roger Leong and Christine Dixon at the National Gallery of Australia have been a fine curatorial team. We congratulate them on their efforts, and say to Roger that his own dream for an internationally focused presentation of Canberra's collection has been admirably realised. We thank the staff of the Gallery, especially those in Conservation, Marketing and Publications, Exhibitions, the Research Library and Photographic Services for such a fine exhibition and publication.

For their generous support, we wish to thank Mrs Diana Ramsay AO and Mr and Mrs T.K.F. Cox.

The support of all the lending institutions is gratefully acknowledged: the St Petersburg State Museum of Theatre and Music, the Victoria and Albert Museum including its Theatre Museum, London, the Musée national d'art moderne—Centre de création industrielle, Paris, the Comité André Masson, Paris, A.A. Bakhrushin State Central Theatre Museum, Moscow, and the Österreichisches Theatermuseum, Vienna.

We wish to thank the specialist contributors to this publication: Lynn Garafola, Natalia Metelitsa, Michelle Potter, the late Nancy Van Norman Baer, and Sarah Woodcock. Their essays discuss the phenomenon of the Ballets Russes from its origins in St Petersburg at the beginning of the century to its legacy as far away as Australia, decades later. To illustrate these essays, selected works from the exhibition have been chosen from among the many splendid costumes and ingenious designs by the foremost artists of the early twentieth century. The impact of the Ballets Russes is still felt today, and with this exhibition and publication we hope to maintain the legacy.

Brian Kennedy   Alan R. Dodge
Director,   Director
National Gallery of Australia   Art Gallery of Western Australia

NTRODUCTION

Between 1909 and 1929 the spectacular productions of Serge Diaghilev's Ballets Russes (the Russian Ballet) transformed the presentation of dance. Diaghilev brought leading modern artists, composers and choreographers together to collaborate on new ballets: the result was an integration of art, dance and music that was unique, and remains influential to this day.

Diaghilev is one of the pre-eminent figures of modern art and culture. The lasting importance of the Ballets Russes is due in large part to his acute sense of timing, extraordinary good taste and judgement. The impresario's productions, for which he conscripted some of the foremost artists of the twentieth century, became a forum for the exchange of new, liberating and often radical ideas. Modern painters found another means of expression: three-dimensional, public, and appealing to new audiences. Unlike traditional painting and sculpture, their creations were not static, but rather depended on the movement of the dancers.

The history of music in the first quarter of the twentieth century would be considerably poorer without Diaghilev's involvement. Through his Ballets Russes he brought the work of the Russian composers Alexander Borodin, Nikolai Rimsky-Korsakov and Igor Stravinsky to a wider European audience. Diaghilev's commissions helped to launch Stravinsky's career, and included the young composer's revolutionary scores for *Petrouchka* and *Le Sacre du printemps* (The Rite of Spring). Diaghilev also embraced progressive Western European composers including Maurice Ravel, Claude Debussy, Manuel de Falla, Eric Satie and Francis Poulenc.

Within the world of dance the impact of the Ballets Russes was profound. At the beginning of the twentieth century, ballet had reached a low point. In Russia, where the classical tradition was formed and sustained throughout the nineteenth century, the full-length ballets on the Imperial stage were at their most elaborate, yet were uninspired in their execution. As the Diaghilev principal dancer, Tamara Karsavina recalled:

> The technique was excellent ... But it was static; the only medium of dancing was toe dancing, and they never went beyond that. Also the Imperial Ballet stood isolated from her sister arts. [Marius] Petipa created wonderful masterpieces but they were done on very mediocre music. The decor too was very ingenious, with most wonderful theatre devices, fountains on the stage, wonderful traps and appearances, transformations and all that, but it had no artistic value whatsoever.
>
> ... in Western Europe the ballet had degenerated into a kind of revue.[1]

In Paris ballet was usually confined to intervals at the opera, while in London performances took place at music halls between the main acts. Diaghilev arrested the malaise by introducing an evening-length program of three or four short ballets, contrasting in theme, music and design. The colour, exuberance and originality of the Ballets Russes caused a sensation amongst audiences accustomed to uninspiring music, predictable choreography, standardised backdrops and costuming.

The Ballets Russes nurtured five of the most innovative choreographers of this century: Michel Fokine, Vaslav Nijinsky, Léonide Massine, Bronislava Nijinska and George Balanchine. Audiences were enthralled

by the ability of Diaghilev's dancers to combine technical brilliance with dramatic expression. Male dance, in particular, was given new prominence and characterisation. The legendary Nijinsky, and other Ballets Russes principals, including Karsavina, Ida Rubinstein, Adolph Bolm and Serge Lifar, became international stars.

Dance is ephemeral, yet the Ballets Russes left a rich material heritage, ranging from original music scores to the brilliant sets and costumes that are the most tangible reminders of Diaghilev's experiments in artistic collaboration. These works, with the artists' original drawings, are now valued as important works of art. *From Russia with Love* presents this art as a window into the world of the Ballets Russes.

(opposite) **Nicholas Roerich** Set design for *Danses polovtsiennes du Prince Igor* Victoria and Albert Museum, London © V & A Picture Library; (above) **Nicholas Roerich** Costume for a Polovtsian warrior in *Danses polovtsiennes du Prince Igor* National Gallery of Australia, Canberra; (left) **E.O. Hoppe** Bolm in *Danses polovtsiennes du Prince Igor* from *Studies from the Russian Ballet* National Gallery of Australia, Canberra

FROM RUSSIA WITH LOVE

Over its twenty-year existence, the designers of the Ballets Russes absorbed and revitalised many of the artistic influences that preoccupied Europe, ranging from late nineteenth-century Symbolism and Art Nouveau to twentieth-century Modernism and Art Deco. In the five years leading up to the First World War, Diaghilev's friends, in particular Léon Bakst, Alexandre Benois and Nicholas Roerich, who were drawn mainly from the St Petersburg *World of Art* (*Mir iskusstva*) group,[2] were predominantly responsible for the appearance of the company's productions. They created images of exotic escapism, revived a world of romantic fairytales, and introduced the folklore of early Russia. In the decade following the war, through the involvement of avant-garde painters such as Natalia Goncharova, Michel Larionov and Henri Matisse, productions by the Ballets Russes came to epitomise Modernist experimentation and Parisian sophistication. These four broad themes form the basis of the exhibition, *From Russia with Love*: Exoticism, Fairytales and tradition, Russian folklore and Modernism.

Exoticism

The success of the company's exotic productions can be linked to the Western European fascination with 'the Orient' as remote, strange and exciting. Tales of sexual passion, high drama and violent death were set in imaginary locations inspired by Persian, Indian, Central Asian and ancient Egyptian cultures. Léon Bakst was the principal designer of these ballets. Their distinctive and vivid colour combinations — jade green, purple, crimson, scarlet and orange — became Bakst's trademark. *Cléopâtre* (1909) was the first of the exotic ballets to be seen outside Russia. This ballet was a reworking of Michel Fokine's 1908 production *Une Nuit d'Egypte* (Egyptian Nights) for which Bakst had also designed the costumes. Its mix of bold, richly patterned design and the theme of seduction and death proved to be such a powerful and popular formula that it remained in the company's repertoire for many years (illus. pp.28, 31). Encouraged by the success of *Cléopâtre*, Diaghilev presented *Schéhérazade* in 1910. In this tale from *The Thousand and One Nights*, Bakst's sensational colour combinations, his fluid, sensuous costumes and shimmering set of monumental proportions heightened the drama of Michel Fokine's expressive choreography and Nikolai Rimsky-Korsakov's atmospheric music (illus. pp.74–9). Paris responded to *Schéhérazade* with great enthusiasm, a response which reverberated across the wider world of the arts, especially theatre, fashion and interior decoration.

In 1912 Fokine and Bakst worked together on two further ballets with Oriental themes: *Thamar* and *Le Dieu bleu* (The Blue God). *Thamar* is set in a castle in Georgia, where Queen Thamar eagerly awaits the arrival of unsuspecting men whom she seduces and then murders. Her costume was designed to bewitch — a fanciful concoction of lilac, blue and cream hues, and studded silk lamé. Both designer and choreographer conjured up a Central Asian mood in the heavily embellished, crimson and blue silk uniforms and the energetic folk dances of Thamar's guards. *Le Dieu bleu* was intended as a lavish showpiece for Nijinsky's talents. Fokine's choreography drew on the classical poses of Indian sculpture as well as the dances of the Royal Siamese court,[3] while Bakst was encouraged 'to excel himself, to produce his most fantastic, his most Oriental'[4] set and costumes. He devised a fantasy land of the Far East, with lavishly ornamented costumes inspired by the colourful imagery associated with the Hindu gods (illus. pp.40–3). Nijinsky's costume was the most brilliant of all: a tunic of printed silk, jewel-coloured satins and watermarked faille with embroidered

silk and golden threads, coloured glass beads and gelatin discs imitating mother-of-pearl.

Bakst's passion for the art and polychrome decoration of ancient Greece influenced the nature of the company's three 'Greek' ballets. His drawings for *Narcisse* (1911), of energetic, barefooted youths and maidens wearing provocatively draped, classically-inspired gowns, prefigured the frenetic and joyous dances created by Fokine (illus. pp.60, 61). The costumes for *Daphnis et Chloé* (1912) are amongst Bakst's finest (illus. pp.44, 45). His use of geometric pattern, such as chevrons and chequerboard motifs, may be traced to the decoration found on ancient Attic vases.[5]

(left) Program cover: *Comœdia Illustré* 1912: Queen Thamar and the Prince in *Thamar*, costumes by Bakst National Gallery of Australia Research Library, Canberra; (opposite) **Léon Bakst** Costumes for Queen Thamar and a guard in *Thamar* National Gallery of Australia, Canberra

9

The simplicity of line, striking decoration and strong colour combinations of Bakst's designs for *Daphnis et Chloé* are in marked contrast to the extravagant ornamentation of his costumes for *Schéherazade* and *Le Dieu bleu*.

L'Après-midi d'un faune (The Afternoon of a Faun) in 1912 was Nijinsky's first attempt as a choreographer. He was guided by Bakst who suggested arranging the dancers as if they were figures on a Greek sculptural frieze. Bakst's set, an Arcadian glade, was placed so far forward on the stage that it limited the dancers' movements to a frieze-like plane (illus. p.63). To the languid flow of Claude Debussy's *Prélude*, the dancers' static poses and angular gestures were an enigmatic accompaniment. Nijinsky played the Faun, whose sexuality is aroused by the arrival of a group of nymphs in the woods. At the conclusion of the ballet, the overtly erotic actions of the Faun caused a scandal at the premiere performance.[6]

Fairytales and tradition reinvented

Nostalgic stories of magic, romance and tragedy were told anew to a sophisticated audience. *Le Pavillon d'Armide* (Armida's Pavilion) of 1909 was originally presented at the Maryinsky Theatre, St Petersburg in 1907. The story is set in France where the images woven into a Gobelin tapestry magically come to life. Alexandre Benois's ornate set and costumes reflected his fascination with the Baroque and Rococo styles of the seventeenth and eighteenth-century court at Versailles (illus. pp.24–7). Choreographed by Fokine with a score by Nicholas Tcherepnine, the ballet was enthusiastically received, although its reception in Paris was overshadowed by the greater novelty of *Danses polovtsiennes du Prince Igor* (The Polovtsian Dances from Prince Igor) that season.

Benois had his greatest triumph with *Petrouchka* (1911). This tragic tale of the love-sick puppet was the most famous and most often revived of all the ballets produced by Diaghilev. With infinite detail Benois created the scene and the characters of the St Petersburg fairground during the Shrovetide festivities of 1830. The interplay of the angular decor, with its slanted perspectives and pitched roofs, and the abrupt, anti-classical patterns of Fokine's choreography found their resonance in the discordant sounds and irregular rhythms of Igor Stravinsky's music. Nijinsky gave an extraordinarily convincing performance as the puppet, Petrouchka, while Fokine's crowd scenes invested the *corps de ballet* with a dramatic energy rarely seen in theatre (illus. pp.36–8).

For *Carnaval* (1910) Fokine's dancers took the roles of the familiar figures to be seen in carnivals and masquerades. First performed in St Petersburg earlier in 1910, this ballet develops the characters associated with Robert Schumann's suite of piano pieces, *Carnaval* op.9, including Harlequin, Columbine, Pantaloon and Pierrot, as well as Chiarina and Euzebius (the composer's fictional names for his wife, Clara Schumann, and for himself).[7] Against Bakst's understated set, the costumes, and therefore the characters, appeared as cameos, but it was the ensemble effect of the entire cast which invested the ballet with its vitality and carnival atmosphere.

In 1921, after many years absence from the Ballets Russes, Bakst was commissioned by Diaghilev to design a revival of the late nineteenth-century classic, *The Sleeping Beauty* — a perennial favourite of the Imperial theatre, renamed *The Sleeping Princess* for the company's London season. No expense was spared. Bakst used strong jewel-like colours for the designs of the hundreds of opulently detailed costumes, creating a magnificent spectacle with the entire cast carefully arranged on stage (illus. pp.66–8). *The Sleeping Princess* retained most of the original choreography by Marius Petipa, the creator of the Russian classical style fairytale ballets. In contrast to the one-act ballets which Diaghilev had popularised, this was the first time that a full-length production, demonstrating the high standard and range of classical ballet, had been seen outside Russia. It was, however, Diaghilev's most expensive undertaking and almost bankrupted the company.

(opposite) **Léon Bakst** Costume for Queen Thamar in *Thamar* (detail) National Gallery of Australia, Canberra
(above) **E.O. Hoppe** Bolm and Karsavina in *Thamar* from *Studies from the Russian Ballet* National Gallery of Australia, Canberra

(above left) Alexis Bulgakov as Pierrot in *Carnaval* Kochno Archives, Bibliothèque nationale de France, Paris; (above centre) **George Barbier** *Carnaval* from *Designs on the Dances of Vaslav Nijinsky* National Gallery of Australia Research Library, Canberra; (above right) **Léon Bakst** Costume design for Chiarina in *Carnaval* St Petersburg State Museum of Theatre and Music; (opposite) **Léon Bakst** Costume for Chiarina in *Carnaval* National Gallery of Australia, Canberra

From Russian folklore to the avant-garde

Productions that drew on the company's native Russian traditions and folklore, embellished and exaggerated, intrigued European audiences. Aleksandr Golovin and Nicholas Roerich, painters who were actively involved in the revival of Russian folk art at the end of the nineteenth century, produced several of these evocative glimpses of early Russia. *Danses polovtsiennes du Prince Igor* — from the second act of Alexander Borodin's opera — was the hit of the Ballets Russes's first season in Paris in 1909. Audiences revelled in the exuberant music with its stirring choruses, accelerating pace, pounding drums and clashing cymbals. The vigorous dances of the maidens and the warriors, in particular Adolph Bolm's virile display as the Polovtsian chief, reinforced the popular image of the Russians as primitive at heart. Little was known of the dances of the Tartar tribes to which Borodin's score refers, and Fokine's powerful rendition was probably more imaginary than authentic. Roerich's designs reflected his own keen interest in early Russian history and folk art, and many of the costumes used the vibrantly coloured warp *ikat* silks of Russia's Central Asian regions. The set refers to the scene in the opera — an evening amongst the camp of the Polovsti. The barren landscape dotted with earth-brown tents against a tawny sky matched the untamed spirit of the ballet (illus. pp. 6, 7).

The 1910 production of the Russian legend, *L'Oiseau de feu* (The Firebird) was praised by contemporaries for its exemplary synthesis of dance, design and music.[8] The score, the first work by Stravinsky to be heard outside Russia, was commissioned by Diaghilev, and Fokine worked closely with the composer to structure the choreography in concert with the music. Golovin's costumes stencilled with patterns in subtle hues of green, pink, blue, beige and mauve were adaptations of the ornate motifs of traditional Russian craft techniques — embroidery, wood carving and painting (illus. pp.34, 35). Intricate patterning also decorated the backdrop, adding to the profusion of varied detail, sound and movement. Bakst designed the costumes for the leading roles of the daughter of the Tsar and the plumed Firebird, danced by Karsavina in one of her most famous roles (illus. pp. 32, 33).

Le Sacre du printemps (1913) marked the Ballets Russes's entry into the world of modernity. Stravinsky's score largely ignored conventions of harmony, rhythm and form, and Nijinsky, as choreographer, reversed almost every convention of classical dance — elegant line, deportment and elevation gave way to awkwardness, trembling and stamping of the ground to call forth the hostile rumblings of nature.[9] The libretto was the result of a close collaboration between Stravinsky and Roerich, the designer. Roerich's geometric patterns, crudely stencilled onto the dancers' robes, were inspired by the motifs of Russian folk costume and provided Nijinsky with ideas for the arrangement of the dancers (illus. pp. 14,15). The ballet provoked an uproar at its Paris premiere, when a confrontation took place amongst the audience, between outraged conservatives and ardent supporters of the new.[10]

While *Le Sacre du printemps* was a difficult engagement with modernity, *Le Coq d'or* (The Golden Cockerel) — Rimsky-Korsakov's opera presented as an opera–ballet — offered another way forward. The company's newest designer, Natalia Goncharova, devised an extraordinary array of Russian folk motifs, odd perspectives and strange proportions. Bright colours and bold floral patterns festooned every surface. Whilst seemingly naïve, her designs were in fact the artist's contemporary use of a 'Neo-primitive' style[11] which drew on folk and popular art forms from her national culture (illus. pp.47, 48).

The character of the Ballets Russes began to alter noticeably during the war years as the success of productions such as *Le Coq d'or* in 1914 signalled the demise of the exotic ballets that had dominated the repertoire to that time. Goncharova and her life-partner, Michel Larionov, who were both leaders of the Moscow avant-garde, replaced Benois and Bakst as Diaghilev's chief artistic advisers. They steered the company away from its St Petersburg origins towards further involvement with artists of the European vanguard. Between 1914 and 1922 Goncharova and Larionov designed several productions. With Stravinsky, Massine and others, such as the French writer Jean Cocteau, they prompted Diaghilev to give commissions to leading modern painters. Collaborators included Henri Matisse, Pablo Picasso, Sonia and Robert Delaunay, André Derain and Georges Braque, as well as the Surrealists Joan Miró, Max Ernst and Giorgio de Chirico, and the Russian Constructivists Naum Gabo, Georgi Yakulov and Pavel Tchelitchev.

Diaghilev's conversion to Modernism was publicly announced in 1917 with *Parade*, Cocteau's ballet, with Cubist designs by Picasso and Erik Satie's strikingly individual score. The young Francis Poulenc wrote: 'I wanted music to be clear, healthy and robust — music as frankly French in spirit as Stravinsky's *Petrushka* is Russian. To me, Satie's *Parade* is to Paris what *Petrushka* is to St. Petersburg.'[12]

Another Modernist ballet, *Chout* (The Buffoon), designed by Larionov, had been commissioned in 1915 although not staged until 1921. In this audacious production, Larionov pushed Russian folk art into a bizarre relationship with the disjunctions of Cubism and the dynamic of Futurism. For many of the costumes, stiffened fabrics were used, and sometimes cane, to realise the distorted, angular shapes which transformed the dancers into living sculptures, unifying them with the jagged forms of the decor (illus. pp.70–3). Serge Prokofiev's music, combining folk tunes and jazz rhythms, was an appropriate accompaniment. The choreography, devised by Larionov with the dancer Thadeé Slavinsky, was considered the weakest element of the work. For some critics, Larionov's design dominated the choreography to the detriment of the ballet.[13] Diaghilev defended this innovation:

> In fact, a new principle has been introduced, that of giving to the decorative artist the direction of the plastic movement, and having a dancer simply give it choreographic form. Both the setting and the music of this ballet are of the highest modernity …[14]

Embracing the spirit of change, Diaghilev commissioned young artists to give a contemporary face to several of his ballets. Robert

Delaunay designed new sets and Sonia Delaunay a number of new costumes for the 1918 revival of Bakst's *Cléopâtre*. Her bold use of contrasting colour equalled the exuberance of the Bakst originals while introducing a clean, modern look (illus. p.30). For the company's New York premiere of *Sadko* (1916), Goncharova redesigned the costumes using the original dream-like set of the 1911 Paris production by Boris Anisfeld. Compared to Anisfeld's delicate and ethereal designs,

(far left) **Nicholas Roerich** Costume design for a maiden in *Le Sacre du printemps* A.A. Bakhrushin State Central Theatre Museum, Moscow; (left) **Nicholas Roerich** Costume design for a youth in *Le Sacre du printemps* A.A. Bakhrushin State Central Theatre Museum, Moscow (opposite) **Nicholas Roerich** Costume for a maiden in *Le Sacre du printemps* Theatre Museum, Victoria and Albert Museum, London/ © V & A Picture Library

Goncharova's costumes were bright and fanciful — fantastic sea creatures, including a number of spectacular golden seahorses, created a kaleidoscope of submarine colour and pattern (illus. p.18). Goncharova was commissioned to redesign *L'Oiseau de feu* for its London season in 1926. Again, her vibrant and boldly detailed costumes lent the production a gaiety not present in the original work.

A common trait of Diaghilev's ballets in the post-war years was the combining of traditional themes with the playful choreography of Massine and the cool eye of modern French painters. For *La Boutique fantasque* (The Magical Toyshop), a witty remake in 1919 of a nineteenth-century German ballet *Das Puppenfee* (The Fairy Doll), Diaghilev engaged the French painter Derain for the design. 'It was on the whole the most painter-like décor we had seen — in contrast to the purely decorative treatment that used the background merely as a foil.'[15]

The successful involvement of artists such as Picasso and Derain encouraged Matisse to accept Diaghilev's commission for the rendering of Stravinsky's opera *Le Rossignol* into a ballet, *Le Chant du rossignol* (The Song of the Nightingale) (1920). Matisse was determined to provide an image far removed from the extravagant world of the earlier Oriental ballets. His striking design — formal, aloof and very French — epitomises the mood of the Ballets Russes in the post-war period (illus. pp.50, 52, 53).

By the middle of the 1920s, these close involvements with painters, musicians and poets living in Paris had significantly altered the character of the company. Diaghilev was increasingly influenced by a more youthful circle of advisors. His secretary and librettist, Boris Kochno, is said to have been responsible for the company's associations with young French artists and composers;[16] although Diaghilev's creative authority was never in abeyance. His production of *Ode* (1928) — along with *La Chatte* (The Cat) and *Le Pas d'acier* (Steps of Steel) (1927) — was truly innovative. In the hands of the designer Pavel Tchelitchev, librettist Kochno, composer Nicholas Nabokov and choreographer Massine, the ballet became a modern, technological allegory of the mysterious forces of nature as represented by the Aurora Borealis. Instead of the standard painted backdrops and curtains, Tchelitchev used a cinema screen, where images of plants growing, horses galloping and people dancing provided an ever-changing, moving 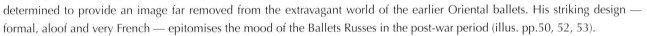 decor. Rows of puppets, mimicking the crinolined dancers, were suspended behind the action. The dancers were enclosed within an irregular framework of white cords, an effect reinforced by tubes of white neon light against which the movement created a succession of shifting geometrical patterns.[17] Tiny mirrors sewn onto the star costumes reflected the light, and there was an added radiance produced by the barium paint decorating the costumes of the constellations (illus. pp. 22, 23). Perhaps too revolutionary for most audiences, *Ode* had only one season. A critic observed: 'there are ... moments when it achieves a sort of original beauty, which in turn produces a peculiar emotional effect'.[18]

Le Bal (The Ball) was one of the company's last productions. The scenario relates the experience of the Young Man who attends a masked ball and is playfully deceived by the guests. The design by Giorgio de Chirico is a Surrealist fantasy in which architectural motifs painted on the backdrop also appear on many of the dancers' costumes, thus reinforcing the theme of deception and ambiguity. The stage was animated not only by the dancers' movements but also by the moving fragments of architectural detail on their costumes — columns, capitals, pediments, brickwork, arches and friezes (illus. pp.16, 17). Balanchine's choreography, in keeping with the light-hearted tone of Vittorio Rieti's music and de Chirico's design, was lively and acrobatic.[19] Within weeks of the end of the 1929 season, in which *Le Bal* premiered, Diaghilev fell gravely ill. He died on 19 August, while on holiday in Venice.

THE LEGACY OF DIAGHILEV

The Ballets Russes disbanded immediately after Diaghilev's death. Several new companies took revivals of the most popular productions around the world, in some cases using the original sets and costumes. Many of Diaghilev's dancers and choreographers formed companies in Europe and North America: George Balanchine and the New York City Ballet, Ninette de Valois and London's Royal Ballet, Serge Lifar and the Paris Opera Ballet, Marie Rambert and the Ballet Rambert, are some of the more enduring ventures. Each tried to keep alive Diaghilev's vision of ballet as a collaboration between various branches of the arts.

For many Australians, one of the most important heirs to the Diaghilev legacy is the company known as Les Ballets Russes de Monte Carlo, which was formed in 1932 by Colonel W. de Basil and René Blum.[20] In its various incarnations the enterprise, which came under the sole directorship of de Basil in 1935, employed a number of the original Diaghilev collaborators including Kochno and the painters Goncharova, Benois, Miró, Derain and Tchelitchev. Several former Diaghilev principals were engaged, including Leon Woizikovsky, Alexandra Danilova, Anton Dolin and Lubov Tchernicheva, the latter becoming the troupe's resident dance teacher.

With access to the original Diaghilev sets and costumes, the de Basil company was able to revive over twenty ballets from the Diaghilev repertoire. De Basil also commissioned new productions which called on the joint efforts of leading artists and choreographers. One of the earliest, and most controversial, triumphs was the symphonic ballet *Les Présages* (Destiny) (1933). The choreographer Massine set his innovative work to Tchaikovsky's Fifth Symphony and presented, in abstract themes, man's struggle with destiny. Massine worked closely with the designer, French Surrealist painter André Masson, who created a stunning backcloth of burning colour, sweeping lines and curves which intensified the energetic fusion of classical ballet and modern dance.[21] Balanchine was the new company's first choreographer, followed by Massine, Nijinska, Fokine and Lifar, while Serge Grigoriev continued in the role of *régisseur général*.[22] Grigoriev's appointment was crucial to the revival of works from the Diaghilev repertoire, due to his extensive experience and accurate memory. The presence of these Diaghilev veterans ensured a direct link to the recent past. It was this legacy which was handed on to ballet in Australia when de Basil's company toured here on three occasions between 1936 and 1940. A remarkable record of these tours was created when a Melbourne eye specialist, Dr J. Ringland Anderson, filmed a large number of the company's performances from each of the three tours.[23] Taken usually from the sidelines, these silent films are mostly in black and white although some later performances are in colour. As the historian Kathrine Sorley Walker notes, 'most ballets and most dancers are represented, and although no ballet is taken right through from beginning to end, there are substantial sequences from many of them. The overall impression is of astounding vitality, energy and commitment'.[24]

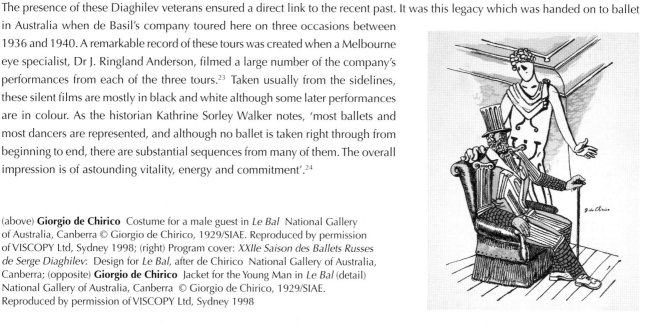

(above) **Giorgio de Chirico** Costume for a male guest in *Le Bal* National Gallery of Australia, Canberra © Giorgio de Chirico, 1929/SIAE. Reproduced by permission of VISCOPY Ltd, Sydney 1998; (right) Program cover: *XXIIe Saison des Ballets Russes de Serge Diaghilev*: Design for *Le Bal*, after de Chirico National Gallery of Australia, Canberra; (opposite) **Giorgio de Chirico** Jacket for the Young Man in *Le Bal* (detail) National Gallery of Australia, Canberra © Giorgio de Chirico, 1929/SIAE. Reproduced by permission of VISCOPY Ltd, Sydney 1998

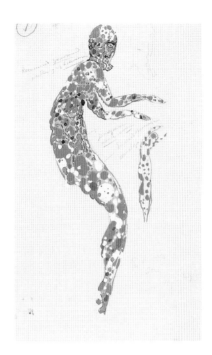

(opposite) **Natalia Goncharova** Costume for a seahorse in *Sadko* National Gallery of Australia, Canberra © Natalia Goncharova, 1916/ADAGP. Reproduced by permission of VISCOPY Ltd, Sydney; (above left) **Natalia Goncharova** Costume design for a seahorse in *Sadko* Victoria and Albert Museum, London/ © V & A Picture Library; (above centre) **Boris Anisfeld** Costume design for the Golden Fish in *Sadko* St Petersburg State Museum of Theatre and Music; (above right) **Boris Anisfeld** Costume design for the Mermaid in *Sadko* St Petersburg State Museum of Theatre and Music

COLLECTING THE ART OF THE BALLETS RUSSES

Costumes are the strength of the National Gallery of Australia's holdings of Ballets Russes material. That so many of these works found a home in Canberra is a testament to the considerable foresight shown in 1973, when nearly one hundred costumes and two backcloths were purchased by James Mollison (the National Gallery's founding director) at the last of three large auctions in London, organised by Sotheby's. The most inspiring aspect of this story is how these objects, and others like them — with all the common ailments of stage properties, such as sweat-stains, ripped and shredded cloth, multiple alterations and hasty repairs — have come to rest safely as fragile works of art in the vaults of theatre, dance and art museums.

The dispersal of the Ballets Russes material began immediately after Diaghilev's death in 1929. Serge Lifar, the principal dancer, and Diaghilev's secretary Boris Kochno were the initial sources of the many drawings, original photographs and archives which found their way into collections around the world, notably the Wadsworth Atheneum, Hartford, Connecticut, and the Bibliothèque nationale de France in Paris. A large number of the costumes, stage properties and musical scores were bought in 1930 by Léonide Massine in the hope of reviving the company. Unfortunately, as the effects of the Wall Street stockmarket crash of 1929 began to spread, Massine's backers withdrew their support and, in 1931, left him as the sole owner of the material. Massine was forced to sell and, within two years, ownership passed to a foundation linked to Les Ballets Russes de Monte Carlo, the troupe formed by Colonel W. de Basil and Réne Blum in 1932.[25] These costumes and sets enabled the new company to revive many ballets from the Diaghilev repertoire over the next two decades. After the death of de Basil in 1951, the property came under the control of de Basil's lawyer, Anthony Diamantidi. As Massine had done, Diamantidi tried and failed to find the financial backing to start a new ballet company. The costumes and sets languished in a warehouse on the outskirts of Paris as years of dust, cold and damp, as well as the financial burden of storage, took their toll.

In 1967 Diamantidi, who was then in his eighties, decided to sell the entire collection at public auction. Sotheby's engaged the Diaghilev historian, Richard Buckle, to supervise the cataloguing. The task involved weeks of unpacking, shifting, piling up and sorting out 'the hundreds of baskets and trunks and bundles' amidst incredible amounts of dirt and dust.[26]

Enough material for three sales was uncovered. Everything was then re-packed, and transported to London. The first sale, which included works by Picasso, Matisse, Braque, Bakst and Goncharova, was held at the (now demolished) Scala Theatre, London, on the evening of 18 July 1968. The former Diaghilev dancer, Lydia Sokolova, choreographed the young dancers who modelled the costumes on stage against the backdrops. This was the last time that many of these costumes would be worn 'live', let alone by a trained dancer. Lighting and music added to the theatricality of the occasion which had become a social event, attracting 'crowds of brightly dressed young people'.[27] The excitement of the sale drew strong bidding on behalf of a group of British buyers who secured many works for London's Theatre Museum of the Victoria and Albert Museum. Other major buyers were The Dance Museum, Stockholm, the Los Angeles County Museum of Art, the Wadsworth Atheneum and The Theatre Museum, Amsterdam. The most outstanding private bidder was Lord Howard of Castle Howard, near York in England. A further sale, held on 19 December 1969, this time at the Theatre Royal, Drury Lane, London, included curtains and costumes by Delaunay, Goncharova, Benois, Roerich, Bakst and Larionov. Strong bidding came from museums in England, the United States and Sweden as well as individual collectors.[28] A third auction was held in London at the Chenil Galleries, Chelsea, on 3 March 1973. Less attention was given to the staging of the sale itself. The National Gallery of Australia was one of the strongest buyers at this auction, purchasing some four hundred items, spread over forty-seven lots, for the modest sum of just over £3,000.

The relatively low-key nature of the third auction reflected the view that many of the best items had been sold previously and that this later sale consisted mainly of incomplete bits and pieces, as well as many costumes from the de Basil Ballets Russes rather than the Diaghilev company. It is true that, among the lots purchased from this sale, there are a number of superb costumes made for productions exclusive to the de Basil and Blum company — ballets such as *Les Présages* (1933). However, through a combination of astute judgement and, perhaps, sheer good luck, a substantial number of these costumes now in the National Gallery's collection have not only proven to be Diaghilev originals, but are among the most coveted items of the period. These include costumes designed by Matisse for *Le Chant du rossignol*, Larionov for *Chout*, Bakst for *Daphnis et Chloé* and *The Sleeping Princess*, and Golovine and Goncharova for *L'Oiseau de feu*, as well as early works from ballets such as *Le Pavillon d'Armide*, *Danses polovtsiennes du Prince Igor* and *Schéhérazade*.[29] Precise attribution and dating of the costumes is made difficult when the same ballets were performed by both companies, as many costumes were constantly altered, repaired or remade. It has taken over twenty years to research, conserve and, in some cases, restore a substantial number of these costumes.[30] The process continues.

The artists' designs for the costumes and sets have long been the most highly sought after elements of the Diaghilev heritage. For many, these drawings offer the least compromised view of the designers' original ideas. The set designs recreate an effect lost to time, while the costume designs, unlike the costumes themselves, contain references to the most fleeting element of the performances — that of the dancer in movement. There is also the more conventional attraction of the drawings considered as works of art able to be framed and hung on a wall. Not surprisingly, many museums as well as private collectors around the world acted quickly after Diaghilev's death to secure the drawings. The purchase of Ballets Russes material at the 1973 auction steered the National Gallery of Australia towards the selective acquisition of drawings. Already, by this time, the scarcity of premium works all but precluded the building of a representative collection of designs. Nevertheless, fortuitous acquisitions have been made, including designs by Bakst for *Schéhérazade*, Benois for *Petrouchka*, and Goncharova for *Le Coq d'or*, as well as drawings by Derain for *La Boutique fantasque* and Juan Gris for *Les Tentations de la bergère* (The Temptations of the Shepherdess) (1924).

Auctions of ballet and theatre material provide a regular opportunity to enrich the collection. The breathtakingly beautiful tunic, designed by Bakst and worn by Nijinsky in the lead role of *Le Dieu bleu,* was bought at auction in 1987, while private sale and gift have brought into the collection costumes designed by Giorgio de Chirico for *Le Bal* and Sonia Delaunay for *Cléopâtre* respectively. The National Gallery's most recent acquisitions were made on 14 December 1995 at the Sotheby's, London, auction for the entire Castle Howard Collection — a seahorse and a squid costume from *Sadko* designed in 1916 by Natalia Goncharova.

Because so many works made for the Ballets Russes are now in museum collections, chances of uncovering even one more gem are increasingly rare. Happily, the result of years of active collecting, researching and documenting has created a world-wide resource with the potential to reconstruct, re-examine and reinterpret the fascinating world of Diaghilev, his company and its followers. The exhibition *From Russia with Love* is the most comprehensive survey of the Ballets Russes to be held in Australia. For the first time, costumes, drawings, posters, photographs and programs from museums and collections in Russia, England, France, Austria and Australia are being reunited with related works held by the National Gallery of Australia. Once again, for a fleeting moment, the art of the Ballets Russes will perform miracles by delighting the eye and enchanting the senses, much as it did in the first half of this century.

Roger Leong

1. Tamara Karsavina interviewed in 1966, in John Drummond, *Speaking of Diaghilev*, London: Faber and Faber, 1997, p.84.
2. See Natalia Metelitsa's essay, 'From St Petersburg to Paris', in this publication pp.24–39.
3. Alexander Schouvaloff, *Léon Bakst: The Theatre Art*, London: Sotheby's Publications, 1991, p.138.
4. Richard Buckle, *Diaghilev*, London: Weidenfeld and Nicolson, 1979, p.222.
5. See Nancy Van Norman Baer's essay, 'Design and Choreography', in this publication pp.40–55, (p.47).
6. The ballet quickly achieved international notoriety, as the prominent headline in an American newspaper declared: 'Wicked Paris Shocked at Last', cited in Nesta MacDonald, *Diaghilev Observed by Critics in England and the United States 1911–1929*, New York: Dance Horizons, and London: Dance Books Ltd, 1975, p.78.
7. Harold C. Schonberg, *The Lives of the Great Composers*, London: Davis-Poynter Ltd, 4th ed., 1977, p.156.
8. M. Henri Ghéon, cited in Serge Lifar, *Serge Diaghilev: His life, his work, his legend. An intimate biography*, London: Putnam, 1940, p.244. Lifar also refers to the critics R. Brussel and A. Bruneau who shared Ghéon's view.
9. Joan Ross Acocella, 'Vaslav Nijinsky', in Nancy Van Norman Baer, *The Art of Enchantment: Diaghilev's Ballets Russes 1909–1929*, exhibition catalogue, San Francisco: The Fine Arts Museums of San Francisco, 1988, p.105.
10. See Buckle (1979), pp.252–3.
11. See Michael Lloyd and Michael Desmond, 'Natalia Goncharova', in *European and American Paintings and Sculptures 1870–1970*, Canberra: Australian National Gallery, 1992, p.101.
12. Cited in Schonberg (1977), p.464.
13. 'I didn't enjoy *Chout* because it didn't seem to me very effective choreographically. And another thing, Larionov had designed the costumes very much in the cubist style, and the costumes and the setting, one rather outshadowed the other. You could hardly see the costumes because of these extraordinary patterns which clashed with the background.' C.W. Beaumont, interviewed in 1966, in Drummond (1997), p.130.
14. *The Observer*, 5 June 1921, cited in MacDonald (1975), p.262.
15. W. A Propert, *The Russian Ballet in Western Europe, 1909–1920*, London: John Lane, 1921, p.53.
16. See Buckle (1979), pp.480–541.
17. Léonide Massine, *My Life in Ballet*, London: Macmillan, 1969, p.174.
18. *The Times*, 10 July 1928, cited in MacDonald (1975), p.361.
19. See Alexander Schouvaloff, *The Art of Ballets Russes: The Serge Lifar Collection of theater designs, costumes and paintings at the Wadsworth Atheneum*, exhibition catalogue, New Haven: Yale University Press in association with the Wadsworth Atheneum, 1997, pp.155–6.
20. De Basil's original name was Vassily Grigorievitch Voskerensky. He was a former Cossack general. The company went by many different names over the course of its life between 1932 and 1951. In 1935 Blum and de Basil ended their partnership. Blum formed another company, the Ballets de Monte Carlo, which, shortly after, was re-formed by Serge Denham into the Ballet Russe de Monte Carlo, with Léonide Massine as artistic director and based in the USA. By 1938 there were two Russian Ballet companies splitting the repertoire and leading dancers, thus adding to the confusion. See Kathrine Sorley Walker, *De Basil's Ballets Russes*, London: Hutchinson, 1982, pp.68, 81–2.
21. Ibid., pp.22–4.
22. The title of *régisseur général*, or production manager, of the Ballets Russes given to Serge Grigoriev (Russia 1883–Great Britain 1968) seriously underestimates his contribution. Grigoriev joined Diaghilev's enterprise in 1909 as a production and business manager. He meticulously carried out Diaghilev's orders and maintained standards for every performance: he supervised the stage and wardrobe staff as well as the condition of scenery and costumes. He joined Col. W. de Basil's Ballets Russes in 1932, serving loyally as its *régisseur* and reproducing the Diaghilev repertoire until the company was dissolved in 1951. Grigoriev's memoirs, *The Diaghilev Ballet 1909–1929* (London: Constable, 1953) is a standard reference.
23. Anderson's films are now in the archive of The Australian Ballet, Melbourne. In Sydney, Dr Ewen Murray-Will filmed a number of de Basil's Ballets Russes performances. The footage is now held at the National Film and Sound Archive, Canberra.
24. Walker (1982), pp.22–4.
25. Schouvaloff (1997), p.31.
26. Richard Buckle, 'Introduction' to *Costumes and Curtains from the Diaghilev and de Basil Ballets*, London: Sotheby Parke-Bernet Publications, 1972, p.xiii.
27. Ibid., p.xv.
28. Ibid., p.xxi.
29. See Josephine Carter, 'Conserving costumes from Les Ballets Russes de Serge Diaghilev', in Robyn Healy and Michael Lloyd, *From Studio to Stage: Costumes and designs from the Russian Ballet in the Australian National Gallery*, exhibition catalogue, Canberra: Australian National Gallery, 1990, p.60.
30. *From Studio to Stage: Painters of the Russian Ballet 1909–1929*, Australian National Gallery, Canberra, 8 December 1990–3 February 1991, was the first major exhibition of this material in Australia.

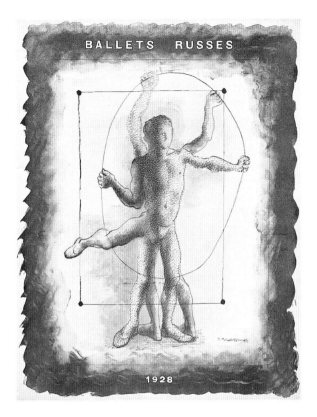

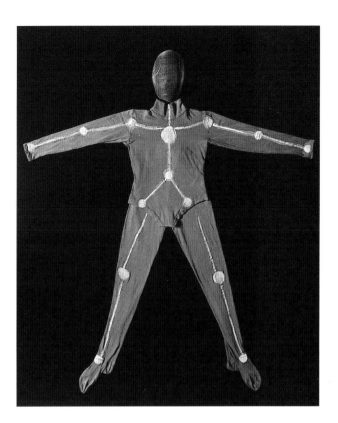

(opposite) **Pavel Tchelitchev** Costume for a star in *Ode* National Gallery of Australia, Canberra; (top left) Program cover: *XXI Saison des Ballets Russes de Serge Diaghilev, Paris* Design for *Ode*, after Tchelitchev National Gallery of Australia, Canberra; (top right) **Pavel Tchelitchev** Costume for a constellation in *Ode* National Gallery of Australia, Canberra; (above) **Lipnitzki** Scene from *Ode* 1928 Kochno Archives, Bibliothèque nationale de France, Paris

ST PETERSBURG TO PARIS

The nineteenth century was slowly coming to an end. 'The Golden Century' of Russian art had introduced the world to Tolstoy and Dostoevsky, Tchaikovsky and Mussorgsky, Repin and Surikov. A new century was dawning, full of anticipation of coming changes in Russia's social and artistic life. Still to come were the cataclysms of the three Russian revolutions and the First World War. But the feeling that old values and old ideals were disappearing was already hovering in the air. Life demanded changes.

In 1890 Serge Diaghilev was eighteen, an energetic rosy-cheeked country boy. He came to the imperial capital of St Petersburg wanting to conquer everyone, his all-encompassing ambition reminiscent of some of the provincial heroes of Balzac and Flaubert.

Diaghilev's artistic beliefs and direction were initially influenced by friends of his cousin, law student Dmitri Filosofov, in whose house in St Petersburg he took rooms. In this city a group of young men who were well educated and talented in various branches of the arts (Konstantin Somov, Eugène Lanceret, Léon Bakst, the musical historian Walter Nouvel, and Alexandre Benois, son of a St Petersburg architect and soul of the party) had founded the 'Society for Self Education', which subsequently became the World of Art (*Mir iskusstva*). Diaghilev absorbed the ideas and debates of his highly educated friends like a sponge. He visited exhibitions and theatres; and in 1895 he toured Europe on two occasions, meeting such celebrities as Emile Zola, Jules Massenet, Charles Gounod and Arnold Böcklin. During this time an entirely different Diaghilev emerged — even his appearance changed: sallow-faced, a showy grey beard, an arrogant glance, impeccably dressed in accordance with his interpretation of a 'Patron of European Style'. But most importantly he was unique in his 'all encompassing creative willingness'.[1] For Diaghilev a period of wide-ranging creativity had begun.

At first it was the World of Art, whose artistic direction had been formulated by 1898 and would actively influence Russian art for

more than two decades. If Benois was the ideological leader of the movement, it was Diaghilev (known as 'Napoleon' and 'Peter the Great' to his friends) who became its organiser. It was Diaghilev who brought the World of Art to the attention of the public: in 1898 he became chief editor of the only art journal in Russia, with the masthead *Mir iskusstva*, and under the auspices of the World of Art he organised five exhibitions of Russian art during 1900–03. Add to this his organisation of the exhibitions of English and German watercolourists (1897); the Scandinavian artists (1898); a monograph written by him about Dmitri Levitsky, the nineteenth-century Russian artist (1902); the grandiose historico-artistic exhibition of more than 2,000 examples of Russian historical portraits (1905); an exhibition of the work of Russian painters in Paris (1906); five Parisian concerts of Russian music (1907); and the grandiose performance of the opera *Boris Godunov* with Feodor Chaliapin in the leading role (1908).

(left) **Alexandre Benois** Costume design for Rinaldo in *Le Pavillon d'Armide* St Petersburg State Museum of Theatre and Music © Alexandre Benois. 1909/ADAGP. Reproduced by permission of VISCOPY Ltd, Sydney 1998; (opposite) **Alexandre Benois** Costume for a musician in *Le Pavillon d'Armide* (detail) National Gallery of Australia, Canberra © Alexandre Benois. 1909/ADAGP. Reproduced by permission of VISCOPY Ltd, Sydney 1998

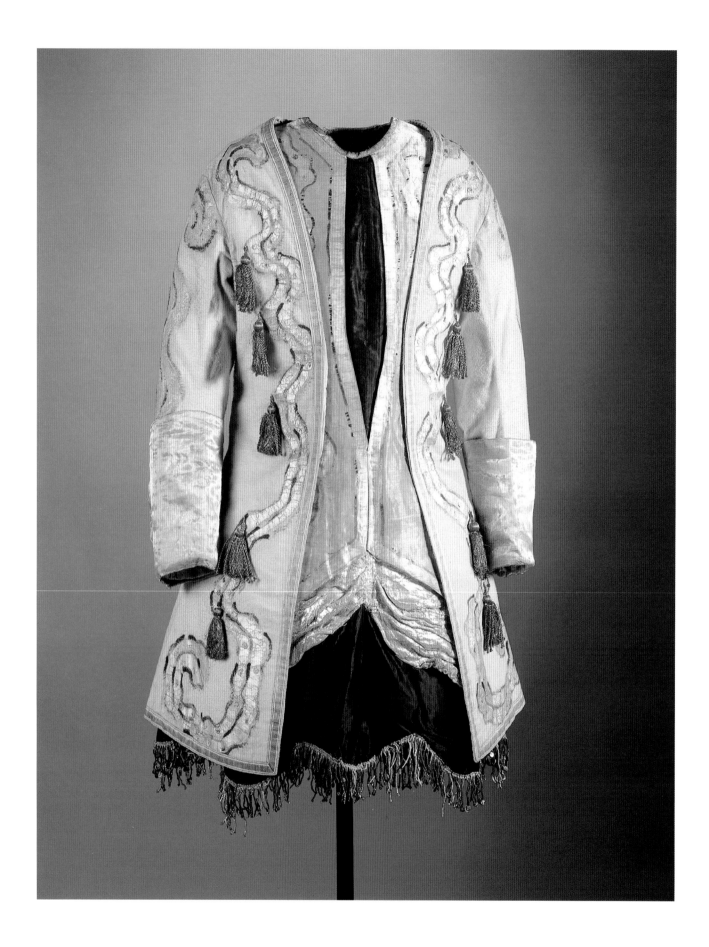

With his gift of artistic intuition — the ability to anticipate what would become new, or to recreate as new the forgotten arts of times gone by — Diaghilev had a vision and perseverance which he brought to bear on every project. The lack of funds did not bother him; on the contrary, it stimulated him. Putting his reputation on the line, captivating his friends, Russian merchants and industrialists with his ideas, he borrowed money and infused it into new projects. He subtly attempted to coerce everyone to his way of thinking. For him there existed only two goals, success and fame, which he would pursue for the rest of his life. Everything that stood in his way, such as friendship or obligations towards near ones and collaborators, was of no consequence to him.

In the initial phases of his artistic development, the theatre was not Diaghilev's main preoccupation, although he joined the civil service in 1899 and entered the Directorate of the Imperial Theatres for Russia. He was commissioned to reform the *Annual Journal of the Imperial Theatres*, which under his editorship became a respected and highly artistic publication.

Diaghilev believed that the theatre was in need of renewed finance and that the hierarchical bureaucracy of the Imperial Theatres impeded the development of the arts. With the cooperation of Prince Serge Volkonsky, who at that time was the director of the Imperial Theatres, and his friends (renowned artists Benois, Bakst, Lanceret and Konstantin Korovin) in 1901 Diaghilev attempted to present the ballet *Sylvia* in St Petersburg's Maryinsky Theatre to the music of Léo Delibes. The performance, envisioned as an innovative production, was never staged. The artists Diaghilev appointed had been brought together without any ideas in common. Volkonsky initially gave Diaghilev *carte blanche*, but the rest of the theatre management soon objected to the concept and insisted that Diaghilev return control to the theatre administration. Diaghilev refused, resulting in a scandal which led to his dismissal and the loss of his right ever to regain government employment.

Not long after this, Michel Fokine, a graduate of the St Petersburg Theatre School and an outstanding dancer, made his appearance at the Maryinsky Theatre. His path would not cross Diaghilev's for another ten years but by then both were ready to search for new approaches to the art of the ballet.

Fokine still had the chance to meet the famous Marius Petipa, who died in 1910. Creator of the grand style nineteenth-century classical Russian ballet, Petipa's monumental fairytale ballets had led to the formation of the national performing school. Their chief feature was the prominence of the female soloist and a powerful *corps de ballet*. Petipa would not accept the fact that his genius was fading, yet he was no longer able to raise himself to his earlier heights as in *The Sleeping Beauty* (1890) and *Raymonde* (1898). In 1903, having created more than sixty productions on the stages of the Imperial Theatres, the famous master left the Maryinsky Theatre with much bitterness.

Fokine's choreographic experiments in 1906, *A Midsummer Night's Dream* set to Felix Mendelssohn's music and the variety show *La Vigne* (The Vine) to Anton Rubinstein's music, were praised by Petipa, who saw in him a successor capable of breathing new life into classical dance.

On 10 February 1907, Fokine staged the ballets *Eunice* and *Chopiniana*. They contained all the fundamental elements of Fokine's mature creations, and together they show the beginnings of two different themes in Fokine's repertoire. As described by the ballet researcher Vera Krasovskaya, 'One may conditionally be called the concept of kinaesthetic dramatisation; the second, the stylisation of a theatrical era gone by.' [2]

The inspiration for *Eunice* derived from images within fine art. The dance appeared as a form of physical illustration of the music. This was immediately commented on by Russian critics, proclaiming Fokine to be 'the colourist of choreography, a poet of lines and splashes of colour'. [3] The themes in *Chopiniana* — the search for the unobtainable ideal, fading beauty, nostalgia for the past — subsequently became Fokine's most loved themes in *Carnaval* (1910), *The Dying Swan* (1907) and *Giselle* (1910). The same themes found expression in the 'Silver Age' of Russian art (1900–10) through different voices — in the prophetic poetry of Alexander Blok and Anna Akhmatova, in the Symbolist experiments of the brilliant young theatre director Vsevolod Meyerhold and in paintings of the World of Art artists, obsessed by the hero as portrayed through the genius of Anton Chekhov, the dramatist.

The meeting of Fokine and Benois was predestined. In 1907 Fokine staged the ballet *Le Pavillon d'Armide* (Armida's Pavilion) at the Maryinsky Theatre, a refined and stylised representation of France in the eighteenth century. This performance became the turning point in the life of the young choreographer, a point of departure and the catalyst for the presentation of the 'Russian Seasons' in Paris. Benois wanted to stage Russian ballet abroad. Knowing of Diaghilev's stunning success with *Boris Godunov* in Paris in 1908, Benois asked him to include some ballet arrangements to create a mixed program of opera and ballet. He saw Fokine, the reformer, as the ballet-master. It was Benois's idea to introduce the yet-to-be-famous choreographer to the impresario, an acquaintance which would vitally influence the future of world ballet in the twentieth century. They met in the autumn of 1908.

A committee, formed to prepare for the 1909 season in Paris, met in Diaghilev's apartment in St Petersburg. As well as Diaghilev, the committee included Benois, Bakst, the composer Nicholas Tcherepnine, the ballet lover and patron Nikolai Bezobrazov, the critics Valerian Svetlov and Walter Nouvel and the *régisseur* Serge Grigoriev.

(left) **Léon Bakst** Costume for a temple servant in *Cléopâtre* National Gallery of Australia, Canberra
(opposite) **E.O. Hoppe** Fedorova in *Cléopâtre* from *Studies from the Russian Ballet* National Gallery of Australia, Canberra

The 1909 operatic repertoire contained *Ivan the Terrible* by Nikolai Rimsky-Korsakov, the first act of *Ruslan and Ludmila* by Mikhail Glinka, and the third act of *Judith* by Alexander Serov. Added were Fokine's one-act ballets *Le Pavillon d'Armide* by Tcherepnine, *Une Nuit d'Egypte* (Egyptian Nights) by Arensky (re-named *Cléopâtre*), *Chopiniana* (re-named *Les Sylphides*), *Danses polovtsiennes du Prince Igor* (The Polovtsian Dances from Prince Igor) and *Le Festin,* a suite of Russian dances consisting of fragments from Petipa's ballets and dances from operas. All these performances, with the exception of *Danses polovtsiennes du Prince Igor*, had already appeared in the Maryinsky Imperial Theatre in St Petersburg.

Diaghilev, the creator and author of the ballet's repertoire, did not put himself forward as such. He did not yet know what his ballet would look like but he did know exactly what it would not be. His ballet had to amaze and enchant the Parisian public. His ballet had to be free of all 'blemishes' of the past — no prefabricated, hastily assembled decorations and costumes, dreary music and imitative choreography. Diaghilev attempted to reconstruct the ballets from his own understanding of the artistic life peculiar to Paris, to make them the new standard in taste.

Cléopâtre was most favourably received. Diaghilev proposed to get rid of everything which seemed to him to represent the aesthetics of the nineteenth century. In this re-working of Fokine's 1908 production of *Une Nuit d'Egypte*, Diaghilev replaced much of Anton Arensky's score with fragments of music from other composers. It became Fokine's task to re-create the Bacchanalian scene to the music of Alexander Glazunov and compose a grand finale, using a fragment from *Khovanshchina* by Mussorgsky. Bakst painted new 'granite-pink' and 'gloomy-violet like' decorations on which 'purple costumes caught fire, gold shimmered and wigs became black'. [4] But the greatest innovation was Cleopatra's costume. The amateur dancer, Ida Rubinstein, was invited to play the role; the angular line of her body was so reminiscent of Aubrey Beardsley's heroines, with a wantonly bewitching beauty and sky-blue wig. All this turned the Egyptian princess into a vampire-woman, a depraved child of the twentieth century.

Disregarding the creative ardour with which the old play was charged, *Cléopâtre* became eclectic and disharmonised, although it still enjoyed popular success. The first step in the search for new ballet aesthetics was unsuccessful and emphasised the old truth: not even the talented components of a re-working will replace a successful original, one which was integrated and innovative both in its conception and implementation.

Danses polovtsiennes du Prince Igor by Alexander Borodin became one of these unsurpassable originals. The genius of Borodin's music inspired Fokine to create a brilliant equivalent in his choreography. Far from an ethnographical resemblance to Borodin's music, which creates an image of an expanse of a limitless steppe carrying wildly galloping horsemen, a poetic rendering of the Polovtsian figure, designed by Nicholas Roerich, gave birth to Fokine's dances of 'spirited barbarism'. [5] Fokine did not exert the slightest influence over the music, but showed his remarkable talent by expressing its figurativeness through dance. Fokine's indisputable masterpiece, which could be said to be the foundation of modern dance, revealed at least two important components: elements of classical dance and theatrical stylisation of national folk dance integrated into the ballet. Only dancers trained in classical exercises were receptive to every nuance of this type of dance. This is why the stunning success achieved by the soloist Adolph Bolm (who had played the role of Luchnick at the Maryinsky Theatre) was no accident. Conceptually *Danses polovtsiennes du Prince Igor* was the most original and, one could say, the first programmed production of the Parisian season.

(opposite) **Sonia Delaunay** Costume for a slave girl in *Cléopâtre* National Gallery of Australia, Canberra Gift of Elaine Lustig Cohen in memory of Michael Lloyd, 1997 © L & M Services B. V. Amsterdam 980701; (right) **Léon Bakst** Costume for a Jew in *Cléopâtre* National Gallery of Australia, Canberra

The Russian Season in Paris in 1909 was a triumphant success. The performances on the stage of the Théâtre du Châtelet not only became major events in the city's intellectual life but also proved to have a great impact on all aspects of Western culture, not to mention ballet itself, which was directly influenced by the Russian Season for more than a decade. The French audience praised the novelty of the painted theatrical scenery and choreography but their highest praise was accorded to the masterly executions of Anna Pavlova, Tamara Karsavina, Ludmilla Schollar and Vera Fokina. The spectators were staggered by the strength and artistry of the male dancers: the revitalised Vaslav Nijinsky, Michel Fokine, Adolph Bolm, Mikhail Mordkin and Georgi Rosai. The ensemble's integrity and the high professionalism of the Russian *corps de ballet* became the common ground on which the company was judged. 'How were the Russians able to achieve such high levels of mastery, when they have to bow to us when it comes to affairs of art?'[6]

Pleased that this question was being asked, Diaghilev departed a wonder-struck Paris. His personal triumph was inextricably linked with the magic of the Russian ballet. For the rest of his life the ballet remained Diaghilev's all-encompassing passion.

The participation of the artists from the World of Art during the Russian Seasons from 1909–14 represented without doubt the most illuminating and characteristic work of all their artistic endeavours. The integrity of the Russian Seasons was in many instances determined by artistic principles which, spanning many years, were arrived at collectively by the World of Art: first it represented an aspiration towards a synthesis of art and culture as a whole; secondly the 'Westernisation' of the majority of its participants, aspiring to become part of the universal artistic process; and, finally, the desire to present their new ideas through a stylisation of the past. They all rode their own 'hobby-horses': for Benois it was the eighteenth century; for Bakst, the spicy East; for Roerich, pagan Russia; and for Golovin, Russian fairytales.

The aesthetic ideals of the World of Art became both the body and soul of Fokine's productions. Their visual ideas determined the presentation of the ballet and even the dancer was understood to be the moving part of the decoration. Fokine was further influenced by the direction that Russian literature, painting and music in small format — the novella, symphonic poem, the impressionistic study — was taking at that time. His favourite forms were the choreographic miniature and the short one-act ballet.

Schéhérazade and *L'Oiseau de feu* (The Firebird) were the principal performances of the second season of 1910. It was Benois's idea to set the erotic *Schéhérazade* to the music of the symphonic poem of Rimsky-Korsakov. He was not in the least concerned about the incompatibility of his intention with the composer's philosophic concept; Rimsky-Korsakov's music was subordinated to the design. Bakst actively participated as co-author of the libretto and created perhaps one of his best designs. Overwhelming in their contrast were the emerald green walls and scarlet carpets of the harem, the female dancers' green and pink costumes, the orange apparel of the odalisques, the warriors' cloaks in clear blue. This violence of colours and Bakst's fantasy were the main contributors which determined the success of this sensuous drama.

(opposite) **E.O. Hoppe** Karsavina as the Firebird in *L'Oiseau de feu* from *Studies from the Russian Ballet* National Gallery of Australia, Canberra; (above) **Léon Bakst** Costume design for the Tsarevna in *L'Oiseau de feu* St Petersburg State Museum of Theatre and Music

Aleksandr Golovin Costume for an attendant of the Immortal Koshchei in *L'Oiseau de feu* National Gallery of Australia, Canberra

Aleksandr Golovin Costume design for an attendant of the Immortal Koshchei in *L'Oiseau de feu* St Petersburg State Museum of Theatre and Music

Alexandre Benois Set design for the Moor's room in *Petrouchka* National Gallery of Australia, Canberra © Alexandre Benois, 1911/ADAGP. Reproduced by permission of VISCOPY Ltd, Sydney 1998

The latest word in the art of ballet was Fokine's choreography, in which natural gestures were of chief importance. In the orgy scene with Shah Shahriar's wives and his slaves, and in the punishment scene, Fokine employed French wrestling manoeuvres which he had studied in his youth. The actors 'flew, fighting, head over heels from the stairs; fell down head first; hung upside down', as he recalled in his memoirs.[7] But the combination of naturalistic pantomime and the elevated style of conventional dance subverted purpose and organisation. Nevertheless the action was so entrancing, and the music and Bakst's powerful scenery so captured the spectators' emotions, that *Schéhérazade* was a stunning success.

The honour of discovering Igor Stravinsky was Diaghilev's alone. Having heard his *Scherzo* and *Fireworks* at a St Petersburg concert in 1908, Diaghilev immediately decided that this was the person he needed. The young Stravinsky, the son of a famous bass singer of the Imperial stage, was obsessed with the theatre and interested in painting and, notwithstanding his often critical outspokenness, was unreservedly accepted into Diaghilev's circle.

Following Tcherepnine's refusal to compose the music for *L'Oiseau de feu* for the 1910 season, Diaghilev invited Stravinsky to do so. It became a collectively inspired exercise, an ideal of creative collaboration, as recalled with pleasure and delight by Stravinsky, Fokine, Benois and Golovin in their memoirs. The choreography ranged from the *faire de pointes* of Karsavina as the Firebird and the dance of the thirteen bare-footed princesses, to the grotesque movements of the characters of the pagan kingdom, ruled over by the fairytale villain, the Immortal Koshchei. The bond linking them together was achieved through Prince Ivan, performed by Fokine; his intention was to make Prince Ivan look as if he were commenting on the action, and to draw the spectators' attention to the miracles being performed before them.

Another of Fokine's stage productions was added to the 1910 season, although initially it was not the intention to include it. In St Petersburg, Fokine staged a charity performance of *Carnaval* on 20 February 1910. This was in support of Vsevolod Meyerhold, who played Pierrot's pantomime role. Diaghilev included *Carnaval* as a dancing interlude, an elegant trifle, to contrast it successfully with the splendour of the East in *Schéhérazade* and the Byzantine, highly decorated *L'Oiseau de feu*.

(left) **Alexandre Benois** Costume design for a peasant woman in *Petrouchka* National Gallery of Australia, Canberra © Alexandre Benois, *c.*1920/ADAGP. Reproduced by permission of VISCOPY Ltd, Sydney 1998; (centre) **Alexandre Benois** Costume design for a reveller in a pig mask in *Petrouchka* National Gallery of Australia, Canberra © Alexandre Benois, *c.*1920/ADAGP. Reproduced by permission of VISCOPY Ltd, Sydney 1998 (right) Karsavina as the Ballerina in *Petrouchka* St Petersburg State Museum of Theatre and Music

The spectacular success of the second season reaffirmed the well-earned reputation of Diaghilev's company. Karsavina and Nijinsky remained the idols of the public. The enigmatically fascinating Firebird portrayed by Karsavina, and Nijinsky's half-man, half-beast of the golden slave in *Schéhérazade*, thrilled the imagination of spectators and critics. The third season in 1911 was in many respects a decisive one for Diaghilev. The union of like-minded leaders had already developed a schism during the second season. Benois fell out with Diaghilev because the latter had failed to mention him in the program as the co-author of *Schéhérazade's* libretto. Diaghilev, however, was afraid of losing Benois as he thought he could still be of use. And he was right; he invited the artist to take part in staging *Petrouchka*, which, generally speaking, became the emblem of the Russian Seasons.

Petrouchka is a shining example of a synthesis its creators could only have dreamt of in their youth. It was a historical landmark for each of them: 'For Stravinsky it signified the vanguard of a long and brilliant development in the world of music; to Benois the artist-creator it came close to the epitome of his creations and to Fokine — the summit, to be followed by decline.'[8] The eternal and universal hero of buffoons in all countries, Petrouchka identified himself with the symbol of the Russian soul and her immortality. This tragic Russian tale, having brought together, in essence, all new ideas in Russian music, painting and literature, simultaneously presents itself as a grandiose generalisation, as metaphor of a mindless world, severe and indifferent to the suffering of the human soul, which with mocking glee and recklessness slides into a bottomless abyss.

Human passions raged on the stage — which was like a puppet theatre — and provoked a profound response from the Parisian audience. Despite the shortness of the performance, Fokine's choreography was faultless. Each doll-like character had its own individual expressive language. 'The complacent Moor is completely revealed. The unfortunate, forgotten and intimidated Petrouchka, all shrunken, withdrew into himself. Inspiration was taken from life to create a most lifeless puppet-like pantomime, using psychologically based doll-like movements'.[9]

Petrouchka is possibly Nijinsky's best creation. The hero's perfectly embodied gestures — knees together, feet turned inwards, bent back, drooping head, mitten covered hands — revealed the depth of his emotional state. Nijinsky was not only presented as a brilliant dancer but also as a great tragic actor. For him, Petrouchka's image contained many profound and personal intimacies.

The fate of Petrouchka became his own destiny. Petrouchka is unable to endure the competition of an indifferent world and dies unnoticed amid the sounds of a cheerful crowd. Equally swift was the demise of Nijinsky's genius, unable to cope with life, to be resurrected like Petrouchka as the legendary 'God's Clown' forever in people's minds.

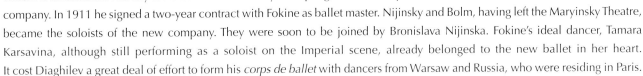

Other ballets of the third season — Tcherepnine's *Narcisse*, and *Le Spectre de la rose* (The Spirit of the Rose) to Carl Maria von Weber's music — appeared as peculiar ornaments to the main event, *Petrouchka*, although they too contained a new tendency. The central theme in both was personified by male and not by female dancers. And, what is more, their ethereal dances, the latter expressing the character of a rose and giving an impression of a flowering and twisting plant, were sensational in the West.

Diaghilev regarded the third season in 1911 as the most important and critical one, following which he affirmed the viability of his beloved creation by attempting to establish a permanent company. In 1911 he signed a two-year contract with Fokine as ballet master. Nijinsky and Bolm, having left the Maryinsky Theatre, became the soloists of the new company. They were soon to be joined by Bronislava Nijinska. Fokine's ideal dancer, Tamara Karsavina, although still performing as a soloist on the Imperial scene, already belonged to the new ballet in her heart. It cost Diaghilev a great deal of effort to form his *corps de ballet* with dancers from Warsaw and Russia, who were residing in Paris.

The 1909–11 seasons may truly be called Russian ones in the history of Diaghilev's company, although the Ballets Russes as such, and Diaghilev's theatrical enterprise, did not adopt this name until after 1911. The ideas and inspiration for the first three seasons derived entirely from Russian art early in this century, fleshed out by Diaghilev's ideas, problems and realisations.

By 1912, however, Diaghilev had already begun to free himself slowly of his like-minded friends who had brought him to world fame. Diaghilev, the charismatic leader, could not bear any opposition. For him other people were important only as carriers of creative ideas. Once they were devoid of ideas, Diaghilev lost interest in them. When he had exhausted both Fokine and Benois, he began to give life to the ideas of Western European creators, to discover new choreographers and dancers.

The Russian heritage that the great impresario tried so ruthlessly to leave behind returned to him in the ever alluring *The Sleeping Princess*, which he produced in 1921 with Petipa's choreography. His most cherished dream was to stage performances of Russian Seasons in Russia herself and gain the acclaim of the Russian public. Fate precluded the realisation of this dream. Diaghilev's company distanced itself further and further from the homeland, only to return in legends and memoirs more than half a century later.

Natalia Metelitsa

1. Alexandre Benois, trans. from *Moi vospominaniia* (*My Reminiscences*), Moscow: Kniga Tret'ya, 1993, p.644.
2. Vera Krasovskaya, trans. from *Russkii baletnyi teatr nachala XX veka* (*The Russian Ballet Theatre at the Beginning of the Twentieth Century*), Leningrad: Iskusstvo, 1971, p.177.
3. Valerian Svetlov, 'Eunice', 'Chopiniana', 'Walpurgis Night', *Birzjovyo vodomosti* (*Stock Exchange Gazette*), 12 February 1907, p.3.
4. Alexandre Benois, trans. from 'Russian Performances in Paris', *Rechi* (*Speech*), 171, 25 July 1909, p.2.
5. A. Gidoni, 'Theatre and dance', trans. from *Petrburgskaya gazeta* (*Petersburg Gazette*), 320, 21 June 1910, p.11.
6. G. de Pavlowsky, 'L'enthousiasme', *Comœdia*, 608, 1909, p.2.
7. Michel Fokine, trans. from *Protiv techeniia* (*Against the Tide*), Leningrad: Iskusstvo, 1981, p.243.
8. Krasovskaya, (1971), p.367.
9. Fokine, (1981), pp.286–7.

DESIGN AND CHOREOGRAPHY
Cross-influences in the Theatrical Art of the Ballets Russes *

The Ballets Russes was not the first to explore a synthesis of arts on stage. Distinguished painters had designed for the theatre since the Renaissance. By the late nineteenth century however, it had become conventional for ballet costumes and sets to be created by skilled artisans working in accordance with established formulas. Russian impresario Serge Diaghilev departed from this practice by commissioning some of the leading avant-garde artists of the time to design the productions of his famed Ballets Russes. During his company's early seasons (1909–14), Diaghilev exclusively engaged Russian artists to design operas and ballets. All had been members of *Mir iskusstva* (the World of Art) and shared its progressive ideas about painting, music, literature and theatrical production. The revolution in scenographic design that Diaghilev popularised centred on the concept of *Gesamtkunstwerk* (the total work of art), in which decor, drama, music and movement were united into a single, integrated whole. Originally formulated by Richard Wagner in the mid-nineteenth century, this principle of unity of vision was brought by Diaghilev and his collaborators to the Ballets Russes stage.

Léon Bakst is the best known of Diaghilev's Russian designers; his sensuous, exotic art characterised the early Ballets Russes performances. Bakst viewed ballet as a continually changing sequence of pictures in frames, and he conceived his costumes and decors as a series of thematically related tableaux.[1] His sumptuous and provocative designs were depicted in carefully organised drawings, and their detailed draughtsmanship revealed a technical mastery of colour and line. As Bakst wrote to Diaghilev in 1911, 'my *mises-en-scène* are the result of a very calculated distribution of paint spots against the background of the decor'.[2]

Bakst designed four major ballets — *Cléopâtre* in 1909, *Schéhérazade* in 1910, and, in 1912, *Le Dieu bleu* (The Blue God) and *Thamar* — as well as several minor productions with costumes and sets inspired by the Far East. Prior to Bakst, costumes for ballets with Oriental themes such as *Le Bayadère* and *La Fille du Pharaon* (The Pharaoh's Daughter) consisted of tutus with fitted bodices and billowing skirts decorated with exotic motifs. Bakst dressed his Oriental dancers in loose-fitting garments such as tunics, boleros, harem pants and split skirts that were closer to the attire of the historical period represented. They also allowed the dancers a wider range of movement, especially in the torso.

Bakst's costumes were as unconventional as the dances of Michel Fokine, the choreographer of most of Diaghilev's pre-war repertory. Fokine sought to extend the line of the dancer's body and to allow increased plasticity and expressiveness through fluid, more natural movement. The bare midriffs of Bakst's costumes for *Le Dieu bleu* allowed dancers to bend freely at the waist, arching backward or curving forward in phrases of dynamic, uninhibited movement. This liberation of body and dress brought a greater psychological naturalism to the ballet stage, creating an expressive picture rather than stilted, conventional realism.

Stylistically, the sinuous line, rich embroidery, and decoratively woven fabrics of Bakst's Oriental costumes reflected Art Nouveau influences from the late nineteenth century. So, too, did Fokine's fluid choreography, especially in the use of the arms 'not to frame the body but to sculpt it three-dimensionally'.[3]

(left) Nijinsky as the Blue God in *Le Dieu bleu* 1912 Kochno Archives, Bibliothèque nationale de France, Paris; (opposite) **Léon Bakst** Costume design for the Sacred Dance in *Le Dieu bleu* Musée national d'art moderne — Centre de création industrielle, Centre Georges Pompidou, Paris

(above) **Léon Bakst** Set design for *Le Dieu bleu* Musée national d'art moderne — Centre de création industrielle, Centre Georges Pompidou, Paris; (opposite) **Léon Bakst** Costume for the Blue God in *Le Dieu bleu* National Gallery of Australia, Canberra

In *Le Dieu bleu*, the constant circling and interlacing of movement patterns of the *corps de ballet* traced graceful, curvilinear forms in space, as did the loose garments, draperies and veils that swirled around them.

Bakst's settings for the Oriental ballets invoked the opulent, decadent world of the legendary East. Vivid pigments, voluptuous interiors and steamy groves conjured up a fantastic world of sensual pleasure and dizzying opium-induced sensations. To stimulate the audience's emotions and fantasies, Bakst relied on colour to evoke exotic, sado-erotic themes. Like many European Theosophists at the turn of the century, he believed in the consonance of specific emotions and colours. He was also familiar with the theories of Russian composer Aleksandr Scriabin, who believed that each musical note had a corresponding colour equivalent.[4] Bakst expressed his views of the subtle and metaphysical power of colour in an interview in 1915:

> I have often noticed that in each colour of the prism there exists a gradation which sometimes expresses frankness and chastity, sometimes sensuality and even bestiality, sometimes pride, sometimes despair … The painter who knows how to make use of this, the director of the orchestra who can with one movement of his baton put all this in motion … who can let flow the thousand tones from the end of his stick without making a mistake, can draw from the spectator the exact emotion which he wants him to feel.[5]

Like a conductor, Bakst 'orchestrated' the constantly changing colour sequences created by dancers in motion. In addition to evoking an emotional response, Bakst's strident colour combinations heightened the passions of the stage drama. Colour and movement worked together to suggest scenes of passionate, uninhibited sex or violence. In *Schéhérazade*, for example, the orgy that forms the climax of the ballet draws the entire cast into a circling, swirling vortex of colour in the midst of which the Golden Slave leaps relentlessly up and down.

(top) **Léon Bakst** Costume for a brigand in *Daphnis et Chloé*
National Gallery of Australia, Canberra
(above) **Léon Bakst** Costume for a brigand in *Daphnis et Chloé*
National Gallery of Australia, Canberra
(opposite) **Léon Bakst** Costume for a brigand in *Daphnis et Chloé*
National Gallery of Australia, Canberra

The tonal relationships between costumes and sets and the striking chromatic chords that Bakst consciously achieved required a close working relationship with a ballet's choreographer. This is not to suggest that Bakst should receive choreographic credit, but the extent to which his designs and ideas about staging and movement influenced a production's choreography should certainly be acknowledged. Bakst's 'Greek' ballets — *Narcisse* (1911), *L'Après-midi d'un faune* (The Afternoon of a Faun) (1912), and *Daphnis et Chloé* (1912) — most clearly demonstrate this interdependence.

Bakst's interest in ancient Greece dated from the 1890s when, as a student in Paris, he often visited the city's museums, particularly the Musée du Louvre.[6] Bakst was also familiar with the antiquities collection at the Hermitage Museum in St Petersburg and, as a member of the World of Art, knew Vasily Rozanov's essays on ancient civilisation published in the group's magazine. In 1907 Bakst spent a summer sketching and studying in Greece with World of Art colleague Valentin Serov and returned anxious to incorporate his vivid impressions into a theatrical production. He had already designed three Greek tragedies for the Imperial Theatres, but these had been more researched than inspired.

Bakst's designs for *Daphnis et Chloé*, the first Greek ballet commissioned by Diaghilev,[7] corresponded with the prevailing artistic view of Golden-Age Greek culture as rational, ordered and pleasantly pastoral. In *Narcisse* however, Bakst revealed an entirely different side of Hellenic society: its tendency towards passionate excess. Fokine's choreography for these two ballets emphasised qualities similar to those found in Bakst's designs. The movement for *Daphnis et Chloé* is poetic, lyrical and tender, while *Narcisse* contained dances of wild frenzy and intoxicating joy. Like the costumes and decor, the choreography reflected more than one aspect of Grecian temperament.

Because of Bakst's knowledge of ancient art and culture, Fokine naturally deferred to him in staging the Greek ballets. As Bakst explained: 'I had to show [Fokine] scene by scene what needed to be done. Then finally he worked out the dance steps.'[8] In this process, Bakst guided Fokine to the figural poses and groupings found in ancient art, particularly Greek sculpture.

Many of the motifs that appeared on Bakst's costumes were taken directly from Greek vase painting. In *Daphnis et Chloé*, for example, he decorated the costumes for the brigands with chevrons, triangles, chequerboard motifs, and stylised vine and leopard-spot patterns (illus. pp.44, 45), all of which appear on Attic black figure ware. Equally noteworthy is the bold polychromatic style of these costumes. Although their pure colour tones and complete absence of shading have an historical source, Bakst mixed his brilliant yellows, greens, purples, oranges and blues in completely new, often harsh, combinations. The aggressive nature of Bakst's colour harmonies heightened the effect of the brigands' boisterous, pyrrhic dance. Their circling bounds and leaps created a kaleidoscope of colour that underscored the most exhilarating moment of the ballet's action.

The third, and last, Greek ballet produced by the Ballets Russes also bore the imprint of Bakst. Not only did he design the costumes, stage make-up, and decor for *L'Après-midi d'un faune*, choreographed by Vaslav Nijinsky, but he guided the choreographer to the angular poses, rigid stance, and two-dimensional movement that created the ballet's frieze-like effect and were largely inspired by ancient art.[9] The composer Igor Stravinsky described the ballet as an 'animated bas-relief' and explained that 'Bakst dominated this production. Besides creating the decorative setting and the beautiful costumes, he inspired the slightest gesture and choreographic movement.'[10]

Nijinsky's Faun revealed certain striking similarities to Fokine's *Daphnis et Chloé*. Under the Arcadian façade of both lurked the unpredictable human instinct. Because of their disparate choreographic styles however, Nijinsky and Fokine interpreted their Grecian source material differently. Fokine's treatment was lighter and more natural; his lyricism softened the archaic poses which he blended with movements derived from academic technique. Nijinsky, on the other hand, emphasised the angularity and two-dimensionality of the flattened figure. By deliberately fracturing the dancer's classical line, he eliminated virtually all references to the traditional ballet lexicon and invoked the geometricised forms of Cubism. Nijinsky's renunciation of classical technique, his embodiment of bestial eroticism and sophisticated fetishism made Fokine's ballets seem tame. The Faun's costume and make-up emphasised his muscular sensuality, the slant of his eyes, his exotic bone structure, underscoring the apparently instinctual spontaneity of Nijinsky's choreography.[11]

The excitement of Bakst's exotic designs could not be sustained indefinitely, particularly in a society thirsting for novelty and innovation. Ironically, it was Bakst's immense popularity that led to his demise, for as audiences grew accustomed to the audacious colours and 'decadent' aesthetic of Bakst's ballets, Diaghilev began to look elsewhere for new sources of pictorial intoxication. In 1914, turning away from the World of Art designers[12] he had previously engaged, Diaghilev presented a startlingly original ballet–opera with costumes and sets by Natalia Goncharova.[13]

The audience gasped when the curtain rose on *Le Coq d'or* (The Golden Cockerel) on 24 May 1914; they were stunned by the bright primary colours, distorted perspective, and stylised floral motifs of Goncharova's Neoprimitivist set (illus. p.48). In contrast to Bakst's elaborately detailed, sophisticated designs, Goncharova's deliberate crudeness reflected a distinctly Modernist aesthetic that sought artistic truth in supposedly

(opposite) **Natalia Goncharova** Costume for a peasant woman in
Le Coq d'or National Gallery of Australia, Canberra © Natalia Goncharova,
1937/ ADAGP. Reproduced by permission of VISCOPY Ltd, Sydney 1998
(right) **Natalia Goncharova** Costume design for a peasant woman in
Le Coq d'or National Gallery of Australia, Canberra © Natalia Goncharova,
1914/ ADAGP. Reproduced by permission of VISCOPY Ltd, Sydney 1998

primitive antecedents — African masks and Byzantine icons as well as native Russian crafts and folk art. The visual impact of the opening scene was particularly dazzling because the curtain was raised during a blackout, a device that allowed the entire decor to be seen at once. This innovation had been suggested by Goncharova who maintained that costumes and decor 'create both the material aspect and the psychological atmosphere of the [stage] scene, even before the actor [dancer] has made a gesture'.[14]

In addition to delighting the eye, the simplicity and naïve spontaneity of Goncharova's Neoprimitive designs provided a welcome antidote to the lush Orientalism and barbaric splendour that had come to epitomise the Ballets Russes and, for many, the moral decay of the era. Goncharova's outwardly innocent interpretation appealed to a society in which impending war demanded responsible thought and a conscious reassessment of values. But while it was charming and naïve in appearance, *Le Coq d'or* in fact was concerned with the more sensual and wicked aspects of human nature. However, Goncharova's stylised approach and playful interpretation allowed audiences to see only what they wanted to see. By rendering festive folk art designs with a primitive directness, she created a childlike fantasy, pulsating with primal energy. This duality pleased the company's Symbolist-oriented audience while satisfying those who were looking for pure entertainment 'without decadent symbols or complications'.[15]

(above) **Natalia Goncharova** Set design for Act III in *Le Coq d'or* A.A. Bakhrushin State Central Theatre Museum, Moscow © Natalia Goncharova, 1914/ ADAGP. Reproduced by permission of VISCOPY Ltd, Sydney 1998; (left and detail opposite) **Natalia Goncharova** Costume for King Dodon in *Le Coq d'or* National Gallery of Australia, Canberra © Natalia Goncharova, 1937/ ADAGP. Reproduced by permission of VISCOPY Ltd, Sydney 1998

(opposite) **Henri Matisse** Costume for a mourner in *Le Chant du rossignol* National Gallery of Australia, Canberra © Henri Matisse, 1920/Succession H. Matisse. Reproduced by permission of VISCOPY Ltd, Sydney 1998
(left) **Henri Manuel** Scene from *Le Chant du rossignol* 1925 Kochno Archives, Bibliothèque nationale de France, Paris

Le Coq d'or is most significant because it marks a shift in the image of the Ballets Russes. Goncharova's semi-abstract compositions moved the company away from Symbolism and towards a Modernist aesthetic. This is particularly evident in her decors. Here the flattening of space, altered perspective, radically stylised and geometricising forms, and the repetition of ornamental motifs, fragment the stage picture into blocks of pattern and colour, and mimeticism yields to abstraction.

Like Bakst, Goncharova used colour for aesthetic as well as expressive purposes. She maintained that the 'tones of the decor are sustained by the tones of the costume in order that their combination does not contradict the sense of the theatrical vision and that it creates, psychologically and visually, a unity of spectacle'.[16] Goncharova saw costumed figures as anonymous mobile units within the stage picture, as well as separate entities in the dance drama. When set in motion against a painted backdrop, her boldly coloured costumes became formal design elements in the overall stage tableau. Colour-coordinated ensembles faded into and out of the background by virtue of their conscious placement on stage and the dancers' carefully designed movement patterns.

Fokine's choreography for *Le Coq d'or* lacked the invention of Goncharova's designs, although it successfully embodied the expressive possibilities of movement. For example, the dances of the seductive Queen of Shemakhan consisted of semi-classical movements performed with supple arms whose languorous motions 'could strangle as well as caress'.[17] The nature of her role as temptress was dramatised by the queen's undulating retinue, moving — with slanted torsos — in sinuous, winding patterns that furthered the spell of Oriental enchantment. King Dodon, on the other hand, was portrayed as a portly old man whose clumsy steps expressed his inept authority and susceptible emotional state.

Goncharova's costumes, like Fokine's choreography, revealed the individual character of each role. The Queen of Shemakhan's loose-fitting harem pants and lustrous gold lamé girdle called attention to the provocative movements of her hips and pelvis in such a way that 'her bewitchment of Dodon seemed inevitable'.[18] For the king's country folk, Goncharova designed Russian peasant-style costumes decorated with bold appliqué patterns in primary colours (illus. pp.46, 47). These suited the comic, unclassical choreography that Fokine created for the dancers, whose movement supported the burlesqued actions of King Dodon. The maids wore peasant dresses that were 'bunched and formless despite their attractive pattern and colour'.[19] With their faces 'clumsily daubed with red', the dancers 'resembled nothing so much as highly coloured Russian Peasant toys, temporarily endowed with life'.[20] These costumes complemented the dancers' brisk, doll-like movements and both enhanced the satirical element of the story that had been banned in Russia because of its political implications.[21]

Le Coq d'or owed its success primarily to its staging — though some critics found Goncharova's setting 'too overwhelming visually to permit undistracted perception of the beauties of ... [the] dancing'.[22] This imbalance between design and choreography was partially due to Diaghilev's decision to present Le Coq d'or as an opera–ballet with dancers miming the action of the singers who were seated in choral formation on both sides of the stage.[23] This innovative resolution required that Fokine invent mimetic, rather than abstract, movement that conformed closely to the sung narrative. Although Fokine's skilful blending of movement and mime was charming, it was overshadowed by the brilliant colour and primitive fantasy of Goncharova's costumes and sets.

Goncharova designed nine productions for Diaghilev, one of which, Sadko (1916), was a reinterpretation of the 1911 original with sets and costumes by Bakst and Boris Anisfeld. In the redesigned version (choreographed by Adolph Bolm), Goncharova completely hid some performers in a costume construction representing a golden seahorse (illus. p.18). Heavily padded and encased in voluminous silk, the dancer's body became a mobile form within the overall scenic landscape, performing necessarily restricted movements. Goncharova also assisted her lifelong companion Michel Larionov with the costumes for other ballets, including Contes russes (Russian Tales). Larionov's designs for Le Bouffon — eventually staged in 1921 as Chout (The Buffoon) — reflect Goncharova's Neoprimitive influence.

The success of the company's Modernist conceptions, as well as its wartime isolation from Russia, prompted Diaghilev to seek future collaborators among the painters of the European avant-garde. Among others, Diaghilev invited Giacomo Balla, Giorgio de Chirico, Georges Braque, Pablo Picasso, André Derain, Sonia and Robert Delaunay, and Henri Matisse to design new ballets. By placing the work of these painters at the centre of his theatrical productions, Diaghilev established the Ballets Russes as a purveyor — and populariser — of Modernism.

Diaghilev's European artist-designers recognised that the theatrical stage promised wide exposure while enabling artistic experiment. According to his biographer, Alfred Barr, Matisse had no particular interest in ballet, but the success of Picasso's *Parade* (1917) and *Le Tricorne* (The Three-cornered Hat) (1919), and Derain's *La Boutique fantasque* (The Magical Toyshop) (1919), encouraged him to accept a commission from Diaghilev. Matisse agreed, in 1919, to design a new version of *Le Chant du rossignol* (The Song of the Nightingale) after listening to Stravinsky play excerpts from the ballet score.[24] The choreography of Léonide Massine, whom Matisse liked and admired, heightened the painter's enthusiasm for the ballet.

Ironically, though Matisse's early Fauvist paintings had emboldened Bakst's and Goncharova's handling of colour, by 1920, influenced by the luminous daylight of the Côte d'Azur, he favoured a subdued palette that he worked with intellectual rigour. Unlike his pre-war odalisques and Orientalising art, Matisse's design's for *Le Chant du rossignol* used:

> very slight means — a sense of proportion, a little invention, [and] intelligent restraint ... [to produce] something delightfully cool and fresh, and free from the oppressive opulence of conventional Western interpretations of the 'gorgeous East'.[25]

The restrained nature of Matisse's designs disappointed the audience. The public still associated the Ballets Russes with lavish spectacle, a fact that Matisse was well aware of:

> Your Russians wait for violence from me? Not at all. I am going to teach them what is the measuring out of colour, according to the French tradition: two pale colours and a pure white. And that will get the better of all their bawling.[26]

The elegant simplicity of Matisse's designs influenced, and was influenced by, the ballet's streamlined choreography. Both suggested a Modernist sensibility, featuring simplified form and a distancing from source material. Hans Christian Andersen's story 'The Nightingale' is set in China, but the Massine/Matisse ballet, described by the choreographer as a 'formalized Oriental fantasy',[27] takes place in an unspecified exotic land. The chinoiserie that characterises the production evokes a mood and atmosphere rather than establishing a time or place, as would a simulacrum of Chinese art.

In his biography, Massine explained that his study of painted and sculpted forms had taught him the rudiments of choreography. It is not surprising to read that the dances in Le Chant du rossignol were as skilfully structured and harmoniously pleasing as 'a porcelain or a bronze from the Ming Dynasty'.[28] In creating the ballet, Massine readily acknowledged his use of poses, movements and groupings taken from Chinese art, specifically paintings on silk and lacquered screens. The dancer Lydia Sokolova noted that:

> There were some very fine and highly ingenious groupings of men in Le Chant du rossignol. They built themselves up into flat friezes, rather in the way that acrobats do, but their bodies were packed tight and knitted close together, some men on one leg, some upside down resting on a bent arm, some in a kind of hand-stand. These groups suggested to me the grotesque combinations of figures on carved ivory boxes, and I wondered if it was from these that Massine had taken his idea.[29]

Massine's arrangement of dancers in human pyramids belied the depth of the stage, as did the planar surfaces of the decor and — in scene two — the uptilted bed of the emperor. In his treatment of the stage as a pictorial surface, Matisse 'imagined a perspective on a very accentuated, almost vertical, inclined plane. The choreography was ordered in the same spirit'.[30] Massine confirmed this shared point of view: 'I worked closely with Matisse to create a fusion of costumes, decor and choreography, and I found this ballet one of my most successful efforts at collaboration with a designer.'[31]

Matisse, in designing Le Chant du rossignol, envisioned the manner in which individual costumes would interact and combine on stage. The sculptural poses and ensemble movement of the uniformly clad corps de ballet allowed the artist to think in terms of volumetric modelling. Matisse designed geometrically-cut costumes for the mourners and mandarins that deliberately masked the curves of the body, thereby transforming the dancers into the building blocks of Massine's accumulative architectonic structures (illus. pp.50–2). When the costumes were isolated and placed in movement by the figures inside, they became part of an overall fluctuating pattern of stylised shape and colour. The mourners' all-encompassing white felt cloaks and hoods, appliquéd with midnight-blue velvet chevrons and triangles, converted the dancers' figures into planar surfaces — abstract shapes — as did the saffron yellow satin robes of the mandarins. In scene two, matching his choreography to the spare design, Massine caused these alternately shimmering and absorbent surfaces to move 'silently before the pale background ... like spirits passing at dawn ... [as the] pale hand of Death was outstretched over [all]'.[32]

Matisse created fitted costumes for the principal dancers, Nightingale and Death, and a constructed garment for the Mechanical Nightingale, thereby separating the symbolic figures from the human characters in the ballet. In spite of their greater realism and detail, these costumes appear modern alongside the elaborate 1914 versions designed by Alexandre Benois for the Ballets Russes's initial staging of the opera Le Rossignol. In the years that followed, the company provided an increasingly influential forum for the intersection of musical, balletic, and artistic Modernism as Diaghilev ceaselessly recruited new talent.

The creative vitality of the Ballets Russes repertoire — from the exotic productions of the 1910s to the Modernist ballets of the 1920s — substantiates Diaghilev's effectiveness as a catalyst for experiment. Just as he linked East with West, and the nineteenth century with the twentieth, he sought a fusion of design, choreography, and music that established the modern performance stage as a flexible, living vehicle for creative expression.

Nancy Van Norman Baer

1. Mary Fanton Roberts, 'The New Russian Stage; A blaze of colour', *The Craftsman,* 29, 1915, p.265.
2. Letter from Léon Bakst to Diaghilev dated 28 April 1911. Cited by Irina Pruzhan (Proujan), *Lev Samoilovich Bakst*, Leningrad: Iskusstvo, 1975, p.130.
3. Lynn Garafola, *Diaghilev's Ballets Russes*, New York and Oxford: Oxford University Press, 1989, p.38.
4. For an explanation of nineteenth-century theories regarding the affinity among colour, musical tones, and emotions, see Charles S. Mayer, 'The Theatrical Designs of Léon Bakst', Ph.D. diss., Columbia University, 1977, pp.183–6.
5. Bakst cited by Roberts (1915), p.265.
6. In Paris, Bakst studied with the Finnish painter Albert Edelfelt (1854–1905) and occasionally worked at the Académie Julian. For complete documentation of Bakst's activities in Paris in the 1890s see Mayer (1977), pp.15–20.
7. *Daphnis et Chloé* was commissioned by Diaghilev in 1909 and scheduled to premiere in 1911. Because Ravel did not produce the music on time, Diaghilev asked Nicholas Tcherepnine to compose the score for another Greek ballet, *Narcisse*, to replace the postponed *Daphnis*, which was eventually performed in spring 1912.
8. Bakst cited by Serge Lifar, *Serge Diaghilev: His life, his work, his legend*, London: Putnam, 1940, p.193.
9. Although the dancer/choreographer Nijinska saw her brother as the sole creator of *L'Après-midi d'un faune*, Arnold Haskell (*Diaghileff: His artistic and private life*, London: Gollancz, 1935, pp.268–9) attributes the ballet's conception to Diaghilev and Bakst. For a description of *L'Après-midi d'un faune* see Joan Acocella, 'Vaslav Nijinsky', in Nancy Van Norman Baer (ed.), *The Art of Enchantment: Diaghilev's Ballets Russes, 1909–1929*, San Francisco: Fine Arts Museums of San Francisco, 1988, pp.96–111.
10. Igor Stravinsky, *An Autobiography*, New York: Simon and Schuster, 1936, p.56. For a discussion of Bakst's source material, including Vsevolod Meierkhold's 1905–07 experiments in 'static theatre', see Lynn Garafola, 'Vaslav Nijinsky', *Raritan*, 8:1, Summer, 1988, pp.2–6.
11. For a discussion of Nijinsky's ability to create roles that confounded conventional distinctions between male and female, as well as human and animal, see Nancy Van Norman Baer, 'The Appropriation of the Feminine: Androgyny in the context of the early Ballets Russes, 1909–1914', *Stowitts Museum & Library, Essays on the History of Dance*, Pacific Grove, California: Park Place Publications, 1998.
12. Bakst, Benois, Roerich, etc.
13. Alexandre Benois claims that he recommended Goncharova to Diaghilev because he was too busy to design the production himself. Arnold Haskell states that the commission came about because of a chance meeting between Diaghilev and Goncharova's companion, Michel Larionov. See Alexandre Benois, *Reminiscences of the Russian Ballet*, London: Putnam, 1947, p.356, and Arnold Haskell, *Balletomania: The story of an obsession*, London: Gollancz, 1934, pp.307–8.
14. Natalia Goncharova, 'Le Costume Théâtral', trans. from Michel Georges-Michel and Waldemar George, *Les Ballets Russes de Serge de Diaghilev: Décors et Costumes*, Paris: Pierre Vorms, 1930, p.22.
15. Henri Guittard, 'Figaro-Théâtre', *Le Figaro*, 26 May 1914.
16. Trans. from Goncharova (1930), p.22.
17. Cyril W. Beaumont, *The Diaghilev Ballet in London*, London: Putnam, 1940, p.97.
18. Sono Osato, *Distant Dances*, New York: Knopf, 1980, p.146.
19. Beaumont (1940), p.95.
20. Ibid.
21. As the dancer Lydia Sokolova explained, 'It seems easy, in the light of after events, to see in King Dodon the unfortunate spoon-fed Czar; [and] in the beautiful Queen of Shemakhan, who turns out to be an evil enchantress, the Czarina whose counsels hastened the fall of her husband's Empire.' Lydia Sokolova, *Dancing for Diaghilev*, London: John Murray, 1960, p.62.
22. A.V. Coton, *A Prejudice for Ballet*, London: Methuen, 1938, p.194.
23. Diaghilev was swayed in this matter by the advice of Alexandre Benois.
24. Alfred H. Barr, Jr, *Matisse: His art and his public*, New York: Museum of Modern Art, 1951, p.207. Stravinsky's opera *Le Rossignol* was first produced by Diaghilev in 1914 with sets and costumes by Alexandre Benois. The production had only six performances and in 1916 Diaghilev commissioned Stravinsky to adapt the music for a ballet with new designs by Fortunato Depero. Because Depero was late in completing the designs, which were also not suitable for touring, Diaghilev postponed the project, offering Matisse the commission in 1919.
25. R.H.W., 'Matisse and Dufy as Designers', *The Athenaeum: A Journal of English and Foreign Literature, Science, The Fine Arts, Music and The Drama*, 13 August 1920, p.217.
26. Matisse, in Michel Georges-Michel, *Ballets Russes: Histoire anecdotique suivie d'un appendice et du poème de Schéhérazade*, Paris: Editions du Monde Nouveau, 1923, p.31; cited in and translated by Melissa A. McQuillan, Painters and the Ballet, 1917–1926: An aspect of the relationship between art and theatre, Ph.D. diss., New York University, 1979, p.486.
27. Léonide Massine, *My Life in Ballet*, Phyllis Hartnoll and Robert Rubens (eds), London: Macmillan, 1968, p.147.
28. Jean Bernier, 'Le Chant du rossignol', in the souvenir program *Les Ballets Russes à l'Opéra*, January–February, 1920, n.p.
29. Sokolova (1960), p.147.
30. Raymond Cogniat, *Cinquante Ans de Spectacles en France: Les décorateurs de théâtre*, Paris: Librairie Théâtrale, 1955, p.24; cited in and translated by McQuillan (1979), p.215.
31. Massine (1968), pp.147–8.
32. Walter A. Propert, *The Russian Ballet in Western Europe 1909–1920*, London: Bodley Head, 1921, pp.60–1.

* This is a revised and abridged essay originally published in *The Art of Enchantment: Diaghilev's Ballets Russes, 1909–1929*, San Francisco: Fine Arts Museums of San Francisco, 1988.

THE SEXUAL ICONOGRAPHY OF THE BALLETS RUSSES

The Ballets Russes transformed just about every aspect of ballet during the twenty years of its existence. From the art of ballet to its enterprise and audience, nothing was left untouched. In the wake of Serge Diaghilev there could be no question of returning to the past without acknowledging the profound changes wrought or set in motion by his company. This being the case, it is indeed curious that the company's influence on the iconographic representation of ballet has been largely ignored. Although certain images are invoked ad infinitum, they are seldom viewed within the larger context of dance iconography or as conveying certain ideas about gender. In fact, they are prima facie evidence of a newly forged link between ballet and the élite homosexual milieux that were attracted to the Ballets Russes.

Ballet before Diaghilev, especially in the West, was a largely female world. Most dancers were women, including those who partnered them pretending to be young men, and most ballets had heroines as their protagonists. In Paris as in London, female pulchritude was at a premium. 'Young and pretty dancers required immediately', advertised the *Nouveau-Théâtre* in 1897, the same year that *Panorama Paris s'amuse*—an album of photographs of the Opéra's leading dancers—displayed them, according to an announcement in *Figaro*, in a 'hundred delicious attitudes of coquetry, passion, or grace'.[1] It was the great subject of Edgar Degas, this Opéra ballet world of the late nineteenth century, with its evanescent tulle and careless physicality, a ghetto of the feminine off-limits to men, except for the occasional voyeur. Degas was not alone in treating the Opéra this way. However, in the paintings of Georges Clairin (think of his portrait of Virginia Zucchi in the Bibliothèque de l'Opéra) or the drawings of Paul Renouard, the erotic appeal is overt, as it is in posters of the period and the titillating dressing room photographs. The many postcards of dancers suggest the popularity and ambiguous appeal of such images.

The Ballets Russes did not bring an end to this trade in images. It did alter their content and the means by which they circulated. Rather than female, the subject nearly always was male and the image usually published in a limited-edition format. Male dancing was certainly one of the great revelations of Diaghilev's early ballet seasons. However, it was not the 'straights' featured in those seasons — Mikhail Mordkin, Adolph Bolm, Michel Fokine, the two Koslov brothers — who inspired the new iconography,

but rather the sexually ambiguous Vaslav Nijinsky. To be sure, Nijinsky was a magnificent dancer, the star around whom Diaghilev built virtually his entire pre-war repertory. But he was also Diaghilev's lover, the only dancer (with the partial exception of Tamara Karsavina and Ida Rubinstein) to enjoy entrée into the privileged circles in which Diaghilev travelled. Among these was the élite homosexual world of Jean Cocteau and Comte Robert de Montesquieu, Baron de Meyer and Princesse de Polignac, Marcel Proust and Romaine Brooks — the core, 'insider' audience for the albums by George Barbier, Paul Iribe, Georges Lepape, and Robert Montenegro[2] that now borrowed the iconography of 'decadence' and Art Nouveau to 'homoeroticise' the body of the Ballets Russes star.

(left) **George Barbier** Nijinsky as the Golden Slave and Rubinstein as Zobeide in *Schéhérazade* from *Designs on the Dances of Vaslav Nijinsky* National Gallery of Australia Research Library, Canberra
(opposite) **Auguste Bert** Nijinsky as the Golden Slave in *Schéhérazade* from E.O. Hoppe, *Studies from the Russian Ballet* National Gallery of Australia, Canberra

Diaghilev, of course, was no stranger to decadence. In the very first issue of *Mir iskusstva* (the *World of Art*),[3] the journal he founded in 1898 and edited until its demise in 1904, he vigorously defended the movement against accusations of 'degeneracy'. 'Where', he asks, 'was that flowering, that apogee of our art from which we are [supposedly] determined to sink into the abyss of disintegration?'[4] In Russia, as elsewhere, the term decadence had homosexual as well as artistic implications. In 1900 the arch-conservative columnist Viktor Burenin referred in print to Diaghilev's 'ultra-swinish' personal relationship with Dmitri Filosofov, his cousin, lover, and deputy editor. According to the memoirs of Sergei Makovsky and Petr Pertsov, the cousins went to Burenin's residence; when he opened the door, Diaghilev slammed his oversize top hat on the journalist's head, an act that silenced him at least where Diaghilev was concerned.[5] The slurs did not stop Diaghilev. He chose to illustrate one of his earliest essays for *Mir iskusstva*, 'Principles of Art Criticism', with a bucolic scene by Aubrey Beardsley, erstwhile art editor of *The Yellow Book*.[6] With its bold line, stylised manner and marked effeminacy, Beardsley's boyish satyr was a forerunner of many of the images associated with Nijinsky.[7]

These images, most of them published in limited editions or in classy magazines such as *Femina*, *Le Théâtre*, and *La Gazette du Bon Ton*, eroticised Nijinsky's body like a pin-up. It wasn't because they showed him nude (as did the drawings of Emile Antoine Bourdelle and Aristide Maillol[8]) or engaged in sexual activity. Rather, what made his body an object of homoerotic desire was the curving opulence of his hips contrasted with the Gibson Girl slimness of his waist, the soft, fleshy thighs (so different from the dancer's heavily-muscled real ones), the jewellery, the make-up, the coy tilt of the head, the languid, limp-wristed gesture, the nipple bared by a chiton, the peep of underarm hair. Although he is sometimes depicted with Tamara Karsavina, his partner in innumerable Ballets Russes productions, he is most often shown alone. Even at Karsavina's side, however, he appears in the throes of self-absorption, as though her presence were incidental and his real partner lay beyond the frame, among the spectators, whom his artfully averted gaze seems trying to seduce. Only in images with Ida Rubinstein, the deadly *femme fatale* of *Cléopâtre* and *Schéhérazade*, does he seem emotionally engaged, gazing worshipfully at the brazen display of her sexuality, the allure of her exposed breasts, the tresses coiling like serpents, the stillness that spelled availability.[9]

Although homosexuality was certainly in the closet during the Diaghilev period, some writers did comment on the androgyny of Nijinsky's persona. One was Cyril W. Beaumont, whose bookshop on the Charing Cross Road, London, specialised not only in dance books but in literature of the 1890s; indeed, by the time he published the Barbier and Montenegro books on Nijinsky, he was regarded as something of an 'authority on the Bohemian, aesthetic movement in Literature, headed and led by Wilde'.[10] Beaumont's remarks in his introduction to the Montenegro album are startling in their directness:

> Nijinsky is not a man in the true, robust sense of the word. He is always surrounded by some invisible, yet nevertheless susceptible halo. It would seem as if Oberon had lightly touched him with his magic wand at birth. An examination of his *rôles* will show that none are allied with the physical strength and beauty of manhood. The youth in love with his own image in 'Narcisse'; the rose-coloured sprite in 'Le Spectre de la Rose'; the lissom Oriental of the 'Danse Siamoise'. These are not parts for the descendants of Mars and Hercules![11]

(opposite) **Auguste Bert** Nijinsky as the Spirit of the Rose in *Le Spectre de la rose* from E.O. Hoppe, *Studies from the Russian Ballet* National Gallery of Australia, Canberra;
(right) **Jean Cocteau** Poster: Nijinsky in *Le Spectre de la rose*
National Gallery of Australia, Canberra © Jean Cocteau, 1911/ADAGP.
Reproduced by permission of VISCOPY Ltd, Sydney 1998

Beaumont goes on to contrast Nijinsky with Adolph Bolm, 'the true embodiment of manlike vigour and masculine virility'. He recalls Bolm, the company's principal character dancer, as he appeared in his most famous role, the Polovtsian chief in *Danses polovtsiennes du Prince Igor* (The Polovtsian Dances from Prince Igor), a warrior 'mad with triumph and excited with the lust of war', leaping wildly, bow held high while amid arrows 'loosed in sheer frenzy'. '*Rôles* such as [this]', concludes Beaumont, 'are impossible for Nijinsky.'[12]

Although he had a riveting stage presence, Nijinsky was not especially good-looking. This was hardly the case of his successor, Léonide Massine, whom Diaghilev discovered at the Bolshoi, made the star of *La Légende de Joseph* (The Legend of Joseph), and marketed as a beautiful boy as well as his latest discovery. However Massine, although living with Diaghilev for nearly seven years, did not present himself as homosexual. Where Nijinsky had drawn attention to his body, Massine did just the opposite. Indeed, nearly all the roles he choreographed for himself during this period, from the Chinese Conjuror in *Parade* to the Can-Can Dancer in *La Boutique fantasque* (The Magical Toyshop), either masked his body or made it comic or grotesque in some way, more often than not effectively neutering it. In fact, Massine did nothing to capitalise on his good looks. He refused to be a pin-up, gay or straight.

The young men who succeeded him in Diaghilev's affections could not have been more different. For one thing they were savvier: they knew the game and were happy to play it.[13] For another, they had no qualms about flaunting their charms in public. There is a photograph of Anton Dolin as Beau Gosse in the 1924 beach ballet *Le Train bleu* (The Blue Train).[14] He wears an old-fashioned bathing suit, with straps over the shoulders and cut low in front, revealing well-developed pectorals. His gaze is unabashedly direct, not a question, or an appeal, but a statement and a challenge: Here I am, take me. This gaze, strong, direct and seductive, also appears in the pictures of Serge Lifar taken by Man Ray and other photographers in the years that followed. Lifar was Diaghilev's

last leading man, George Balanchine's first Apollo and Prodigal Son, a diamond in the rough remade as a Deco god. All swagger as the Officer in *Barabau* (in some pictures he is shown brandishing a sword), he mugs flirtatiously as the French sailor in *Les Matelots* (The Sailors); in *Roméo et Juliette* he gazes through a harlequin's mask, while in *La Pastorale* he wears a toothy grin and heavy lipstick.[15]

With Dolin and especially Lifar reappear elements of Nijinsky's erotic packaging — the slim waist, the indiscreet nipple, the make-up, the artful pose and gesture. Except that now the image displays a new toughness, the angular, hard-edged look of modern design combined with an insistence on the body's physical musculature. Often the legs are naked, with thongs laced high up the calf; belts cinch the waist; the chest is hairless; the pectorals, abdominals and thighs have the sinewy hardness of an athlete's.

(opposite) **Léon Bakst** Costume design for a Bœotian youth in *Narcisse* St Petersburg State Museum of Theatre and Music; (above) **Léon Bakst** Costumes for a Bœotian youth and girl in *Narcisse* (detail) National Gallery of Australia, Canberra; (left) Anton Dolin as Beau Gosse in *Le Train bleu* 1924 Kochno Archives, Bibliothèque nationale de France, Paris

(opposite) **Léon Bakst** Costumes for nymphs in *L'Après-midi d'un faune* National Gallery of Australia, Canberra; (above top) **Léon Bakst**
Set design for *L'Après-midi d'un faune* Musée national d'art moderne — Centre de création industrielle, Centre Georges Pompidou, Paris
(above left) **Baron Adolf de Meyer** Nijinsky as the Faun in *L'Après-midi d'un faune* 1912 Bibliothèque nationale de France, Paris
(above right) **Baron Adolf de Meyer** Scene from *L'Après-midi d'un faune* 1912 Bibliothèque nationale de France, Paris

Such toughness was not limited to the stage, but reflected — or, at least, paralleled — changes in the homosexual audience at large. Complaining about the 'beautiful burgeoning boys' who crowded London performances of the Ballets Russes in the late 1920s, *Vogue* critic Herbert Farjeon observed:

> The velvet-voiced youth of twenty who has taken possession of the Russian Ballet is more formidable than his aesthetic predecessor of thirty or forty years ago. He is not so drooping, not so languishing, he does not court the interesting pallor of former days. On the contrary, he is surprisingly pink in the cheek, surprisingly fit, surprisingly unready to go down like a ninepin.[16]

Because photographs circulated to a broad audience — the ones in question, for instance, were published in magazines as well as company programs — the expression of homoeroticism was circumspect. However, in limited editions such as Eileen Mayo's album of drawings of Lifar published in England in 1928,[17] the homoerotic content is more explicit. This is particularly noticeable in the drawings based on photographs: in almost every instance they exaggerate the suggestiveness of the pose, the arch of the torso, the pout of the lips, the bulge of a calf, buttock or thigh. In playing up both the butch physicality and the narcissism of the originals, the artist makes Lifar an icon of gay desire.

Like earlier representations of Nijinsky, Mayo's drawings typically depict Lifar alone. In a sense they are only marginally concerned with dance, using it as an excuse for displaying the attractions of a physically active body in motion, of minimising the wantonness of sexually provocative movements performed by men. In fact, they are closer to erotica than dance images, offering a limited number of spectators a source of private delectation. Only 500 copies of the Mayo book were printed, and relatively few of the images were reproduced elsewhere. Four hundred copies of Barbier's book on Nijinsky were printed, and just over 900 of the Iribe–Cocteau volume. Such figures lend support to the argument that with the Ballets Russes the male dancer became a subject of homosexual erotica, just as images of the female dancer had previously figured in its heterosexual counterpart.

In any number of ways the Mayo album harked back to the earlier tradition associated with Nijinsky. The link is evident not only in the format and graphic style but also in the iconography — the feathers, fabrics and props that serve as fetishes, the exposed nipples, the artifice of the surrounding scene, even some of the poses. Indeed, it is hard to believe that Mayo was unaware of Barbier's *Designs on the Dances of Vaslav Nijinsky*. Both books were published by Beaumont, and each contained an essay by him. Here was the beginning of a gay tradition that Carl Van Vechten and George Platt Lynes would pick up and elaborate upon in photography.[18]

To be sure, not all images of Lifar highlighted his virility. Indeed, in 1929 *The Sketch*, a popular London illustrated magazine, published a 'decoration' by Félix de Gray[19] that barely distinguished between Lifar in the title role of *Apollon musagètes* (Apollo) and two of the Muses that served him: all wore pleated, thigh-skimming tunics, looked to the side in profile, had generous hips and limply extended arms. Whereas the Muses gambolled in the background on *demi-pointe*, Apollo stood on full *pointe*, a pose that only underscored his effeminacy, *pointe* work being traditionally the domain of women. In a certain sense, the image neutralised the homoeroticism of Lifar's image by overtly feminising it.

Eileen Mayo Lifar as Boreas in *Zéphire et Flore* from *Serge Lifar* National Gallery of Australia Research Library, Canberra, Feint Collection

While the 1930s witnessed a return to more conventional representations of gender in ballet, the homoerotic tradition associated with the Ballets Russes did not vanish. It simply went underground, becoming a part of the era's burgeoning gay literary and visual culture. Although ballet remains pre-eminently an art practised and consumed by women, it has come to be regarded as a gay art, inherently so in the view of some scholars. Yet, as the sea change in early twentieth-century iconography clearly demonstrates, there is nothing intrinsically gay about ballet any more than there is anything intrinsically straight about baseball. Ballet became a magnet for gay men because of Diaghilev's Ballets Russes, which was not only a showcase for gay male talent and gay male themes, but also a meeting ground where gay men could socialise relatively free of the constraints of the closet. Although for millions of little girls, ballet remains a vision of tutus and Sugar Plums, for gay men it represents — at least in part and largely thanks to Diaghilev — a homoerotic nirvana, where the display of male beauty and desire for the male body can be experienced within the safe haven of high art.

Lynn Garafola

1. 'Petites Nouvelles', *Figaro,* 23 March 1897, p.5; 'Courrier des Théâtres', *Figaro,* 7 March 1897, p.3.
2. See, for instance, George Barbier, *Designs on the Dances of Vaslav Nijinsky,* foreword Francis de Miomandre, trans. C.W. Beaumont, London: C.W. Beaumont, 1913; and Jean-Louis Vaudoyer, *Album dédié à Tamar (sic) Karsavina,* Paris: Pierre Conrad, 1914; Robert Montenegro, *Vaslav Nijinsky: An artistic appreciation of his work in black, white and gold,* foreword by Cyril W. Beaumont, London: C.W. Beaumont, 1913; *Vaslav Nijinsky. Six vers de Jean Cocteau. Six dessins de Paul Iribe,* Paris: Société Générale d'Impression, 1910. For Georges Lepape's Nijinsky drawings, some of which were published in Ballets Russes souvenir programs, see Claude Lepape and Thierry Defert, *From the Ballets Russes to Vogue: The art of George Lepape,* trans. Jane Brenton, London: Thames and Hudson, 1984.
3. See Natalia Metelitsa's essay 'From St Petersburg to Paris', in this publication pp.24–39, for a discussion of *Mir iskusstva.*
4. 'Lozhnye voprosy: Nash mnimyi upadok' (Complicated Questions: Our supposed decline), *Mir iskusstva,* 1: 1–2, 1899, p.3.
5. I am grateful to Simon Karlinsky for this information.
6. *The Yellow Book* was a British illustrated quarterly that appeared from 1894 to 1897. Closely associated with the Aesthetic Movement and Art Nouveau, it published the work of many distinguished artists and writers, including Aubrey Beardsley (who was the art editor), Max Beerbohm, Henry James, Edmund Gosse, and Walter Sickert.
7. The image appeared in 'Osnovy kudozhestvennoi otsenki' (Principles of Art Criticism), *Mir iskusstva,* 1: 3–4, 1899, p.54. Illustrations by and articles about Beardsley appeared in a number of issues, underscoring John Bowlt's contention that the journal revealed 'a distinct predilection for the graphics of Beardsley' (John E. Bowlt, *The Silver Age: Russian art of the early twentieth century and the 'World of Art' group,* Newtonville, Mass.: Oriental Research Partners, 1979, p.63).
8. For reproductions of these nudes, see *Nijinsky, un dieu danse à travers moi,* catalogue of an exhibition at the Musée-Galerie de la Seita, Paris, 15 December 1989–17 February 1990, pp.80, 96, 97; and Claude Aveline and Michel Dufet, *Bourdelle and the Dance: Isadora and Nijinsky,* Paris, Arted, Editions d'Art, 1969, pls 91–4.
9. This is especially clear in Barbier's various treatments of *Schéhérazade.* See, for instance, the two unnumbered plates in *Nijinsky*; 'Mlle Rubinstein, sous les traits de Zobéide', *Le Théâtre,* December 1911, 2, n.p.; 'Ida Rubinstein and Nijinsky in "Schéhérazade"', *Catalogue of Ballet and Theatre Material,* London: Sotheby Parke Bernet, 25 May 1977, lot 35.
10. Quoted in Cyril W. Beaumont, *Bookseller at the Ballet,* London: C.W. Beaumont, 1975, p.88. Beaumont was quoting Annesley Graham, the editor of the short-lived magazine, *The Interlude,* which Beaumont published and to which he contributed two essays, written under the pseudonym Leonard Hamilton.
11. Cyril W. Beaumont, 'Vaslav Nijinsky: An Artistic Appreciation of His Work', in Montenegro, *Vaslav Nijinsky* (1913) n.p.
12. Ibid.
13. Anton Dolin wrote in *Last Words: A final autobiography,* London: Century Publishing, 1985, pp.31–2, which was published posthumously: 'When I went to Paris to audition for Diaghilev in September 1923, I think I realised, though not in a worldly-wise way, what was in store for me there. Diaghilev had made his interest in me apparent, although not overt, during the London season, when I had been a shy youth of seventeen. Now here I was at the age of nineteen, having grown up a little and learned a lot, well developed, and a good enough dancer, I was confident, to join his company as a principal. Somewhere in my mind I knew that this would put my relationship with him on a different footing.'
14. This photograph is reproduced in Boris Kochno, *Diaghilev and the Ballets Russes,* trans. Adrienne Foulke, New York: Harper and Row, 1970, p.217.
15. Most of these photographs are reproduced in the company's souvenir programs. Otherwise, the best collection is to be found in André Levinson, *Serge Lifar: Destin d'un danseur,* Paris: Grasset, 1934.
16. Herbert Farjeon, 'Seen on the Stage', *Vogue* (British edition), 11 July 1928, p.80.
17. *Serge Lifar: Sixteen drawings in black and white by Eileen Mayo,* foreword by Boris Kochno, trans. Sacheverell Sitwell, appreciation by Cyril W. Beaumont, London: C.W. Beaumont, 1928.
18. For Carl Van Vechten, see Jonathan Weinberg, '"Boy Crazy": Carl Van Vechten's Queer Collection', *The Yale Journal of Criticism,* 7: 2 , 1994, pp.25–49; for George Platt Lynes, see James Crump, 'Iconography of Desire: George Platt Lynes and gay male visual culture in postwar New York', in *George Platt Lynes: Photographs From the Kinsey Institute,* introd. Bruce Weber, Boston: Little, Brown, 1993, pp.149–56.
19. 'A de Gray Decoration on a Russian Ballet Theme', *The Sketch,* 3 July 1929, p.22.

IAGHILEV THEATRE

Looking back imposes a pattern on the past, a pattern often not discernible at the time amid the minutiae of everyday living. History discerns clarity where there may have been confusion, a clear progression where those involved were faced with multiple choices, policy where there was only pragmatism, artistic intentions where the driving force was survival. Theatre history becomes a record of first nights, overlooking the daily grind of rehearsal, preparation and the ever-changing nightly performance, whose qualities are dictated by that most unpredictable of creatures — the live audience.

Serge Diaghilev's ballet is rightly seen as a great artistic enterprise, but no theatre company exists for twenty years on artistic principles alone. The director of a ballet company cannot only please himself — he is responsible for the livelihoods of a large number of performers, musicians, backstage staff and administrators, and this affects his policies. The theatre has known many idealists who scorned the commercial aspects of theatre or had no practical, technical or administrative backup to help translate ideas into reality. To be a practical and successful man of the theatre involves many qualities, not least the ability to read the public mood, never to be too far ahead of them, to catch the moment to translate new movements into popular ones, and to evaluate the tastes of different audiences, whether in Paris, London, Barcelona or Manchester. He has to be prepared to survive bankruptcy, to know when to put pragmatism above ideals.

Diaghilev survived because his artistic aims were matched by a practical theatrical mind that enabled him to give substance to the visions of others. But not all his productions had perfect artistic unity and integrity — he embraced compromise if it meant theatrical survival. After the failure of *The Sleeping Princess* in 1921 in London, with the costumes impounded against his debts, and Paris awaiting the new production, he rearranged Act III, decked the wedding guests out in a mixture of *Cléopâtre*, *Le Pavillon d'Armide* (Armida's Pavilion) and new designs by Natalia Goncharova and called it *Le Mariage de la belle au bois dormant* (Aurora's Wedding).[1] He was not only driven by artistic considerations but by the thought 'we open on Tuesday'.

Diaghilev was the right man in the right place at the right time — the greatest piece of luck anyone can have. His ballet hit Western Europe at the point when nineteenth-century realism and a decayed ballet tradition had both run their course and audiences were ready for change. In place of cumbersome, detailed sets and costumes, the designers brought colour, bold shapes and light; in place of tinkly tunes, composers created full-blooded, complex scores; pretty girls (who, in European ballet, often played the male roles *en travesti*) were replaced by women and men of vitality and spirit; where there had been a single style of classical ballet, Michel Fokine revealed the classically-trained dancer as an expressive medium capable of myriad styles and emotions. Audiences were thrilled to the marrow. But Diaghilev did not fall into the trap of repeating the successful formula — the company's repertoire constantly developed to reflect the changing times, although this was also a reflection of Diaghilev's low threshold of boredom.

(left) **Léon Bakst** Costume for the English Prince in *The Sleeping Princess*
Theatre Museum, Victoria and Albert Museum, London/ © V & A Picture Library
(opposite) **Léon Bakst** Costume for a lady-in-waiting in *The Sleeping Princess*
National Gallery of Australia, Canberra

Diaghilev perceived new movements at a point when they were ready for general consumption and translated them into theatrical form — the acceptable face of the avant-garde. The theatre is a potent transmitter. Orientalism had been popular in nineteenth-century art and literature for over half a century, but not until *Schéhérazade* in 1910 did it filter down into fashion and interior design; less than five years later, the first modern blockbuster musical, *Chu-Chin-Chow*, leaned heavily on Bakstian design and introduced Orientalism at a new popular level.[2] Similarly, left to art galleries, Cubism could have taken years to filter into general public consciousness, but given physical form in *Parade* in 1917 it had immediate impact.

Except for intermittent flirtations with the classics — an abbreviated *Swan Lake*, a few performances of *Giselle*, the three-month season of *The Sleeping Princess* and its off-shoot *Le Mariage de la belle au bois dormant* — Diaghilev's ballet repertoire was made up of new works by a succession of choreographers, each of whom revealed another facet of the possibilities of the classically-trained dancer. Some of the ballets became standards; some were ballets of their time and within a few seasons became old-fashioned; others were intentionally ephemeral; others experimental.

Michel Fokine, Vaslav Nijinsky, Léonide Massine, Bronislava Nijinska — choreographer succeeded choreographer. Each seemed irreplaceable, and Diaghilev's genius lay in never substituting a new favourite for the old; for each new marvel, he 'invented' a new type of ballet to suit the new talent.

On looking back it is tempting to analyse the ballets and try to see how closely they reflect the prevailing *Zeitgeist* — to hear the guns of the First World War prefigured in the pounding rhythms of *Le Sacre du printemps* (The Rite of Spring) in 1913 and read into the reports of the seeming chaos of its choreography the death of an old world. How much was conscious and how much unconscious is impossible to say. Certainly it is true that in the mid-1920s, the frenetic desire to be chic and up-to-date reflected the superficiality of the period, but of course Paris had always wanted something new. In the post-war period, Diaghilev consciously provided ballets with local inspiration to interest different audiences on his touring schedule — *Les Femmes de bonne humeur* (The Good-humoured Ladies) (1917) based on Goldoni's play and set to music by Domenico Scarlatti for Rome; *The Triumph of Neptune* (1926) based on toy theatre and with English collaborators for London; *Le Train bleu* (The Blue Train) for Monte Carlo, after the company found a winter base there in 1924. All one can say is that, like any expert successful theatre producer, consciously or unconsciously, Diaghilev knew his audiences and knew his time.

Diaghilev's hand in the creation of these works was practical and always theatrical. He set new standards for ballet music, no longer relying on in-house musicians but commissioning composers as well as adapting existing music of all periods and styles. A musician of taste and discrimination, he could select and edit music by Gioacchino Rossini for *Le Boutique fantasque* (The Magical Toyshop) or Scarlatti for *Les Femmes de bonne humeur*. His understanding of what would work on stage was total and artists of the calibre of Pablo Picasso accepted his criticisms without demur. He was an expert in theatre lighting, could spot faults in the *corps de ballet*, and hear mistakes in the orchestra. He could train a choreographer, select the right man for the right job — teacher, *régisseur*, composer, designer or choreographer. Such gifts for incessant organisation on such a scale equal creation.

Not the least of Diaghilev's revolutions was to establish around 1909 the dominance of the one-act ballet, a concept originally introduced by Fokine. Programs now included three or four works in an evening, which called for a new skill — program building. This entailed constructing a balanced and contrasted evening's entertainment, setting one work against another, new works with standards, comedy against sensation, avoiding works that were too similar in choreographic style, music or design, while ensuring that the dancers had time to make the necessary changes or were not worked too much (although Tamara Karsavina did once dance *Thamar*, *Le Spectre de la rose* (The Spirit of the Rose), *Les Sylphides* and *Carnaval* in the same evening). Also, once the ballet was established as a permanent touring company, the preferences of the different cities had to be taken into account — Paris favoured a constant diet of new works, while London was more conservative and often did not see new works until a year after their creation.

(opposite above) **Léon Bakst** Costume design for the Queen and her page in *The Sleeping Princess* National Gallery of Australia, Canberra; (opposite) **Léon Bakst** Costume for the Bluebird in *The Sleeping Princess* National Gallery of Australia, Canberra (above) **Natalia Goncharova** Costume for an Ivan in *Le Mariage de la belle au bois dormant* National Gallery of Australia, Canberra © Natalia Goncharova, 1922/ ADAGP. Reproduced by permission of VISCOPY Ltd, Sydney 1998

(opposite) **Michel Larionov** Costume for a
buffoon's wife in *Chout* National Gallery of
Australia, Canberra © Michel Larionov, 1921/
ADAGP. Reproduced by permission of VISCOPY
Ltd, Sydney 1998

(far left) **Michel Larionov** Costume design for the
Merchant in *Chout* Victoria and Albert Museum,
London/ © V & A Picture Library © Michel
Larionov, 1915/ADAGP. Reproduced by permission
of VISCOPY Ltd, Sydney 1998

(left) **Michel Larionov** Costume design for the
Chief Clown in *Chout* Victoria and Albert
Museum, London/ © V & A Picture Library
© Michel Larionov, 1915/ADAGP. Reproduced
by permission of VISCOPY Ltd, Sydney 1998

(below) **Michel Larionov** Set design for the
Merchant's garden in *Chout*
Österreichisches Theatermuseum, Vienna
© Michel Larionov, 1921/ADAGP. Reproduced
by permission of VISCOPY Ltd, Sydney 1998

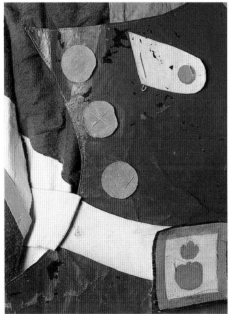

(above and detail) **Michel Larionov** Costume for a soldier in *Chout* National Gallery of Australia, Canberra © Michel Larionov, 1921/ADAGP. Reproduced by permission of VISCOPY Ltd, Sydney 1998 (opposite) **Michel Larionov** Blouse for a bridesmaid in *Chout* National Gallery of Australia, Canberra © Michel Larionov, 1921/ADAGP. Reproduced by permission of VISCOPY Ltd, Sydney 1998

In establishing his own company, Diaghilev lost access to the services that supported the Imperial Theatres in Moscow — the workshops, wardrobe, the school that trained the best dancers in the world. He had to build a team to deal with the myriad unglamorous tasks that make up the day-to-day life of a company throughout the year. This meant planning the repertoire, casting, booking theatres, negotiating contracts, finding scene painters and costumiers, arranging the repair of existing scenery and costumes; noting the box office take, the settling of financial guarantees, paying of salaries, paying of bills, and keeping accounts; engaging and rehearsing an orchestra in each city, arranging storage of works not currently in the repertoire and getting them out again as required. It meant planning the movement of a large company plus costumes and sets across Europe, often to ill-equipped theatres, finding rehearsal rooms, timetabling classes, timetabling rehearsals for new works and rehearsals for revivals or to keep the current repertoire in shape — always allowing time for the dancers to eat or travel between rehearsal rooms and the theatre — taking rehearsals, finding rehearsal pianists, and coping with the incessant demands for money from dancers and suppliers.

Diaghilev did not always go with the company on tour, but remained in constant touch, the telegram as insistent as any telephone or fax, and often as quick. Surviving papers speak eloquently of the day-to-day problems — especially financial. They are littered with final demands, threats of legal action (Diaghilev only paid bills at the very last moment), telegrams from Walter Nouvel or Serge Grigoriev asking for fees to be paid, desperate pleas for him to send money to release baggage from the carriers or costumes from store, asking for approval in cast changes. They are a salutary corrective to anyone who imagines that Diaghilev's life was lived on a high artistic plane.

It is perhaps the surviving costumes that bring us closest to this theatrical reality, and to the glamour of performance. Many bear honourable scars — the hasty repairs alongside more careful darns and patching, the alterations for different dancers, the wear under arms and around belted waists where the sweat has rotted the fabric, make-up clinging to the necks, the many names — the names of the first casts beautifully written on tapes, later ones scrawled hastily on the lining in pencil. Their fabrics and making speak eloquently of the fluctuating finances of the company. Early costumes are of great lavishness, made by the best costumiers in Paris and Russia, of the finest fabrics, decorated with opulent braids mixed with unashamedly theatrical sequins and studs, or imaginatively dyed and painted. Those for *Chout* (The Buffoon) however, are redolent of the financial straits through which the company was passing in 1921; they work on stage but do not bear close examination — like Diaghilev himself, who always looked immaculate, but sometimes had holes in his shoes.

Costumes are, of course, the *raison d'être* for the designs. Today the designs are seen as works of art, complete in themselves, but a design can be artistically satisfying yet not succeed as a costume. They are only a step on the way and do not really exist until pencil and paint have been translated into fabric and decoration, taking into account what a dancer will tolerate and what is possible given the movements they have to make. While *Chout* looks wonderful in display — witty, inventive, and so important for the scholar as an example of emerging Constructivism — on stage the costumes were cumbersome and swamped the choreography; the details could not be appreciated, for the scenery was so complex and colourful that the total effect was muddle and confusion. Léon Bakst's famous designs, all chiffons and bare breasts, looked very different when the bare flesh was translated into heavy jersey (it takes some time to realise that the olive-brown jersey midriffs in some *Le Dieu bleu* (The Blue God) costumes were meant to represent bare flesh, and the dancers' faces and hands were made up to match) and when the costumes were worn by dancers of very different proportions from those of Bakst's fantasies. For some historians, the design is the 'reality'; they disregard the discrepancy between design and finished costume. Yet the costumes were never intended to be seen singly, but in movement, each one with an appointed place in the stage picture — then the designs lived as the designers intended. Our experience now is back to front; we come to the designs *before* the ballets.

This theatrical vibrancy is lost forever. Theatre lives and dies in the instant, and is never the same from night to night — that is its unending appeal and its greatness. It leaves relics, a tantalising jigsaw from which so many pieces are missing, and which now build a very different picture from the original. Diaghilev has become one of the most studied and analysed figures in twentieth-century culture, but the price of the acceptance into academe (and museums) has too often been the surrender of the vital association with the theatre.

Sarah Woodcock

1. Other examples of Diaghilev's pragmatism can be seen in the re-use of *Narcisse* costumes in *Daphnis et Chloé* or the re-use of *Daphnis et Chloé* scenery for *The Gods Go a-Begging* (1928).
2. There is a neat irony in the fact that it was in trying to emulate *Chu-Chin-Chow's* impressively long run, and the resulting financial benefits, that led Diaghilev into his one spectacular misjudgement — the revival of the full-length production of *The Sleeping Princess*.

AVALANCHE: DE BASIL'S BALLETS RUSSES IN AUSTRALIA

Greatest Ballet Attraction in Our Theatrical History!

Such was the advertising that announced the 1936 Sydney season by the Monte Carlo Russian Ballet, the first of three Ballets Russes companies to visit Australia between 1936 and 1940. For Australians, isolated from first-hand contact with European developments in the arts, these visits were momentous. The tours provided audiences with an unprecedented panorama of new visual and aural experiences, from the choreography of Michel Fokine to the music of Igor Stravinsky, from the designs of Natalia Goncharova to the dancing of Tamara Toumanova.

In Adelaide, Brisbane, Melbourne and Sydney, the arrival of the Ballets Russes companies sparked debate. In the local newspapers and in widely-circulated journals and magazines such as *Art in Australia*, *The Home* and *Table Talk*, the discussions centred on a variety of issues including the significance and authenticity of the works Australians were seeing, and the role of the Ballets Russes in fostering well-informed audiences for the arts. The impact of the tours on both the practical development of the performing and visual arts and the maturing of debate about the arts in Australia has, with reason, become legendary.

The companies toured under a variety of confusingly similar names, including the Monte Carlo Russian Ballet, the Covent Garden Russian Ballet and the Original Ballet Russe. But they were all directed, at least in principle, by former Cossack army officer turned entrepreneur, Colonel W. de Basil.

De Basil — who came to Australia only on the third tour, that of the Original Ballet Russe — remains an enigmatic and controversial figure. He was lauded by some as the successor to Serge Diaghilev, put down by others as a poor substitute. Kathrine Sorley Walker says of him:

> Life with him was an intensely human affair of rivalries, ambitions, camaraderie, temperamental outbursts, squabbles and reconciliations — and never dull for a moment.[1]

There are many conflicting ideas and theories about de Basil's directorship of his companies. After the death of Serge Diaghilev in 1929, were the de Basil Ballets Russes companies the renaissance that the ballet world longed for, as an enthusiastic Arnold Haskell implies,[2] or were they, as James Monahan states, not so much a renaissance as an epilogue in the history of dance?[3] Is Walker right in suggesting that de Basil was a disseminator rather than a creator?[4] And what of Jack Anderson's remark that, while de Basil had 'an unquenchable love of ballet', he never formulated a coherent artistic policy nor established long-range goals for his companies.[5]

In many respects, the ideas and theories put forward by English and American scholars about the nature of de Basil's directorship, however persuasive, are simply not important considerations in the Australian context.

(left and detail opposite) **Léon Bakst** Costume for Shah Zeman in *Schéhérazade* National Gallery of Australia, Canberra

At the time of the Ballets Russes tours, Australia's extreme insularity in both a geographical and cultural sense presented an unusual set of circumstances. Although Australian audiences had not been entirely ballet-starved prior to 1936 — there were the tours by Adeline Genée, Anna Pavlova, Olga Spessivtseva and their partners, for example, as well as some local activity[6] — there had never been anything like the Ballets Russes. There had never been such spectacles as the exotic and orgiastic *Schéhérazade*. Nor had there been the extravagance of *Le Coq d'or* (The Golden Cockerel), brought to Australia by the Covent Garden Russian Ballet in 1938. This newly-created version, without the singers of the original Diaghilev opera–ballet, and with more emphasis on the humour of the story, featured the Golden Cockerel as a dancing role. There had never been such a modern approach to choreography as Léonide Massine's symphonic works, *Les Présages* (Destiny), *Choreartium* and *Symphonie fantastique*, and his exuberant *Jeux d'enfants* (Children's Games) with its surreal, slightly quizzical designs by Joan Miró. Nor had there been such displays of artistry and technical skill from dancers of international repute such as Irina Baronova, Hélène Kirsova, Paul Petroff, Tatiana Riabouchinska, Tamara Toumanova, Igor Youskevitch, and a host of others.

Such was the power of the Ballets Russes companies in Australia that their legacy was perpetuated during the decades that followed their visits. Kirsova returned to Australia in 1938 after scoring a major personal success as a leading dancer with the Monte Carlo Russian Ballet between 1936 and 1937. By 1941 she had established the Sydney-based Kirsova Ballet, Australia's first professional ballet company. Then in mid-1939, with the threat of war in Europe looming, a number of de Basil's dancers elected to remain in Australia at the conclusion of the Covent Garden Russian Ballet tour. They included Kira Abricossova, who eventually founded the West Australian Ballet in the 1950s; Edouard Borovansky, whose Borovansky Ballet provided Australian audiences with their main experiences of ballet for over two decades during the 1940s and 1950s; and a group of Polish dancers, including Raisse Kousnetzova, whose Polish–Australian Ballet gave performances in Sydney during the 1940s and 1950s. For dance in Australia the legacy of de Basil's Ballets Russes was immense, and it was not until the 1960s that the strength of this legacy began to wane slightly as English influences began to make themselves felt more strongly with the appointment of an Englishwoman, Peggy van Praagh, as the first artistic director of the Australian Ballet.

(opposite) **Léon Bakst** Costume design for Shah Zeman in *Schéhérazade* National Gallery of Australia, Canberra; (above left) **Léon Bakst** Costume design for an odalisque in *Schéhérazade* National Gallery of Australia, Canberra; (above right) Program cover: *Colonel W. de Basil's Monte Carlo Russian Ballet* 1937 Scene from *Schéhérazade*, after Norman Lindsay National Gallery of Australia Research Library, Canberra

For Australian visual artists and theatre designers the situation was similar. Until the visits by the Ballets Russes, Australians had very little opportunity to see original works by those at the forefront of developments in the visual arts. They mostly had to be content with a few reproductions in books and magazines. The first major show of modern European and British art in Australia, the *Herald Exhibition of Modern Art*, opened in Melbourne in October 1939. It created shock waves, with Salvador Dali's *L'Homme fleur* generating a furore about the merits and demerits of Surrealism, which eventually polarised around James Gleeson's defence and Lionel Lindsay's attack.[7] Yet by October 1939 the Ballets Russes had already visited twice and the opening night of their third tour was imminent. De Basil's designers included Léon Bakst, Alexandre Benois, André Derain, Giorgio de Chirico, Natalia Goncharova, Michel Larionov, André Masson, Joan Miró, Nicholas Roerich and Georges Rouault. By the time the *Herald* show opened, the Ballets Russes companies had already presented a sweep of European art and design in Australia.

There are numerous accounts, from both artists and scholars, of the impact and the influence of the de Basil companies on the Australian visual arts community. Sidney Nolan, for example, was given his first theatrical commission to design a set and costumes for Serge Lifar's restaging of *Icare* (Icarus) for the Original Ballet Russe in Sydney in 1940 (illus. p.83). Nolan often made reference to the impact the Ballets Russes companies, and this particular commission, had on him.[8] Richard Haese, in his study of the development of modern art in Australia, also pays due homage to the influence of the Ballets Russes, pointing out, in particular, that the Ballets Russes helped break down 'Australia's cultural insularity and anglophilia'.[9]

Considering the repertoire that was brought to Australia, it is clear, too, that Australian audiences were not being fobbed off with a second-rate, worn-out product. While some of the ballets that were brought to Australia were treasures from the Diaghilev repertoire, some were also relatively new. The version of *Le Coq d'or* that was presented in Australia in 1938 had been created by Fokine only one year before in 1937, and Massine's first symphonic ballet, *Les Présages*, was seen in Australia in 1936, just three years after its world premiere in Monte Carlo in April 1933.

(above) *Program: Les Ballets Russes Program Officiel édité par Comoedia Illustré:* designs for *Schéhérazade*, after Bakst National Gallery of Australia, Canberra; (left) **Léon Bakst** Costume for an almeé in *Schéhérazade* National Gallery of Australia, Canberra; (opposite) **Léon Bakst** Costume for the Chief Eunuch in *Schéhérazade* National Gallery of Australia, Canberra

Les Présages was contentious even by northern hemisphere standards. Set to Tchaikovsky's Fifth Symphony, the ballet examined man's passions, conflicts and triumphs. The controversy that surrounded it centred mainly on Massine's use of symphonic music. Massine was not the first choreographer to use symphonic music for dance but with *Les Présages*, and with his subsequent symphonic ballets, he developed a way of working in which the dancers represented different themes and different musical instruments. To many music purists, this kind of visualisation of musical structure was an act of heresy.[10] The debate continued in Australia.

Choreographically, Massine made extensive use, unusual for the time, of counterpoint and mass movement, and groupings in both horizontal and vertical arrangements. *Les Présages* was also a departure from the comfortable, in that Massine, while choreographing conventionally classical steps for the dancers' feet and legs, broke the balletic formality of the torso and arms and had the dancers move their upper bodies in a way that recalled the expressive movements of the modern dance.[11] Without expressing disapproval, Igor Youskevitch, who danced in Australia with the Monte Carlo Russian Ballet, called the choreography for *Les Présages* 'grotesque' simply because he could find no other word in his vocabulary to describe the then highly innovative combination of the classical and modern that Massine created.[12] Although there was some modern dance in the European tradition being seen in Australia in the 1930s,[13] audiences did not experience the full impact of the European expressionist style in dance until the 1940s. By then the Viennese modern dance pioneer, Gertrud Bodenwieser, had arrived in Sydney, established a company and a school, and had begun to disseminate her modern Central European choreographic legacy in a determined and structured manner.

Then there were André Masson's designs for *Les Présages* — a front curtain, a backcloth and costumes.[14] Taking up Massine's themes of conflict, turbulence, passion and triumph, Masson's backcloth, in red, green, yellow, purple and brown, juxtaposed symbols of stars and comets against curving organic shapes, and waves and flame-like contours against angular patterns (illus. p.82). His costumes (illus. pp.80, 81) echoed the colours and patterns of the backcloth.

Both backcloth and costumes generated debate from the first performance of *Les Présages* onwards. Walker remarks that in England and Europe they were 'hated and admired almost equally'.[15] Again the debate continued in Australia. At times Masson's designs were praised for their modernity,[16] at times they were ridiculed, with the costumes inciting comments such as 'banal and naïve',[17] and the backcloth being likened to 'a liver on the dissecting table'.[18]

In the early decades of the twentieth century Massine was considered a theatrical innovator by such arbiters of taste as Guillaume Apollinaire, Clive Bell and T. S. Eliot, and for Australian audiences in 1936 *Les Présages* provided an insight into Massine's way of working and collaborating. Visually, musically and choreographically, *Les Présages* was a new artistic experience to which Australians responded enthusiastically. *Les Présages* was shown in every Australian city visited by the Ballets Russes companies. It received 116 performances during the touring period 1936–40, and in terms of sheer numbers of performances it was outclassed only by predictable audience-pleasers, namely *Le Mariage de la belle au bois dormant* (Aurora's Wedding), *Le Spectre de la rose* (The Spirit of the Rose), *Swan Lake* Act II and *Les Sylphides*.[19]

(opposite) **André Masson** Costumes for two women from Scene 2 in *Les Présages* National Gallery of Australia, Canberra © André Masson, 1933/ADAGP. Reproduced by permission of VISCOPY Ltd, Sydney 1998; (right) **André Masson** Jacket for a man from Scene 1 in *Les Présages* National Gallery of Australia, Canberra © André Masson, 1933/ADAGP. Reproduced by permission of VISCOPY Ltd, Sydney 1998

 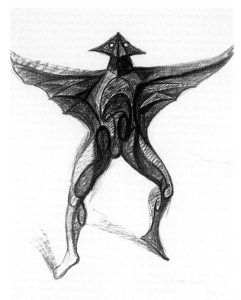

(left) **André Masson** Design for the set and wings for *Les Présages* Fondation André Masson, Paris; (right) **André Masson** Costume design for Fate in *Les Présages* Fondation André Masson, Paris © André Masson, 1933/ADAGP. Reproduced by permission of VISCOPY Ltd, Sydney 1998 (opposite) **Sidney Nolan** Set design for *Icare* National Gallery of Australia, Canberra © Courtesy of Jane Glad

The effects of *Les Présages* continued to resound in Australia. Borovansky staged a production called *Fifth Symphony: Les Présages* for his Borovansky Ballet in 1955. The choreography was by Yurek Shabelevsky, who had been in Australia with the Covent Garden Russian Ballet in 1938, and the piece was designed by William Constable. But Borovansky found himself having to manage a law-suit when Massine was rightly outraged that, as Edward Pask puts it, the Shabelevsky *Présages* was 'little more than a carbon copy of Massine's *Les Présages*'.[20] Even earlier in 1940, when William Constable designed costumes for the female *corps de ballet* in *Vltava*, Borovansky's choreographic meditation on his homeland of Czechoslovakia, he surely had Masson's costumes in *Les Présages* in mind. The long, slim, reed-like patterns that curve upwards from the hemline of Constable's softly-falling dresses for *Vltava* recall quite clearly the designs of Masson's costumes.

Les Présages was not, of course, the only work brought to Australia by de Basil's Ballet Russes to have a major impact. Other works that received much exposure over the full touring period, and enjoyed great popularity with Australian audiences, included *Danses polovtsiennes du Prince Igor* (The Polovtsian Dances from Prince Igor) (91 performances), *Carnaval* (89 performances), *Schéhérazade* (81 performances), and *Petrouchka* (71 performances). Although none suffered the litigious fate of the Borovansky production of *Les Présages*, many of these popular works were restaged in Australia in subsequent years, often by former de Basil dancers, especially for the Borovansky Ballet and the short-lived but influential National Theatre Ballet Company in Melbourne.

The photographer Max Dupain, commissioned by publisher and patron of the arts, Sydney Ure Smith, to photograph the Ballets Russes dancers for various publications, has referred to the 'avalanche of dancing' that the touring companies brought with them to Australia.[21] It was an avalanche not just of dancing but of design and choreographic innovation as well. If de Basil was a director without long-range goals and a coherent artistic policy, in the Australian situation it was of little consequence. Whether he encouraged a renaissance or inaugurated an epilogue is similarly unimportant. The Australian arts community was eager to be astounded when these chic, glamorous dancers arrived with their very European repertoire. Australians were receptive and the Ballets Russes gave them more than they could have hoped for.

Michelle Potter

1. Kathrine Sorley Walker, 'De Basil', in *International Dictionary of Ballet*, Martha Bremser (ed.) Detroit: St James Press, 1993, p.354. For further discussion of the controversial figure of de Basil see Kathrine Sorley Walker, *De Basil's Ballets Russes*, London: Hutchinson, 1982, chapter 2: 'The Colonel'.

2. Arnold L. Haskell, *Balletomania: The story of an obsession*, London: Gollancz, 1934. See especially chapter 12: 'Home Again — Les Ballets Russes de Monte Carlo'.

3. James Monahan, *The Nature of Ballet: A critic's reflections*, London: Pitman, 1976, p.iv.

4. Walker (1982), p.222.

5. Jack Anderson, 'The Ballets Russes Saga', *Ballet News*, January 1982, p.15.

6. For an overview of ballet in Australia before 1936 see Edward H. Pask, *Enter the Colonies Dancing: A history of dance in Australia 1835–1940*, Melbourne: Oxford University Press, 1979.

7. See James Gleeson, 'What is Surrealism?' *Art in Australia*, 81, 25 November 1940, pp.27–30 and 'The Necessity for Surrealism', *Comment*, 5, May 1941, and Lionel Lindsay, *Addled Art*, Sydney: Angus and Robertson, 1942, pp.27–33.

8. See Rosemary Neill, 'Nolan at 70', *Bulletin*, 21 April 1987, pp.70–4 and Jane Clark, *Nolan: Sidney Nolan landscapes and legends*, Sydney: ICCA, 1987, p.34. Nolan's work for *Icare* is discussed in Michelle Potter, 'Spatial Boundaries: Sidney Nolan's Ballet Designs', *Brolga*, 3, December 1995, pp.53–67.

9. Richard Haese, *Rebels and Precursors: The revolutionary years of Australian art*, Ringwood, Vic.: Allen Lane, 1981, p.96.

10. Articles by Ernest Newman, music critic for *The Times* (London), who supported Massine's use of symphonic music, were published in *The Times* in July and August 1936. Replies to his articles by another music critic, J.A. Westrup, giving a different opinion, appeared in the *Daily Telegraph* (London). Newman's articles are collected in Ernest Newman, *Symphonies and Ballets: Six articles reprinted from the London Sunday Times*, New York: Hurok Attractions, 1938.

11. *Les Présages* has been remounted by former de Basil dancer Tatiana Leskova for a number of companies including the Dutch National Ballet, the Joffrey Ballet and the Paris Opera Ballet. Films of some of these restagings are available in the Dance Collection of the New York Public Library. Footage of *Présages* in Australia was shot by Sydney dermatologist, Dr Ewan Murray-Will, and is accessible to the general public through the National Film and Sound Archive, Canberra.

12. *The Art of Léonide Massine: Symphonic ballets*, [videorecording] New York: ARC Videodance, 1989. Dance Collection, New York Public Library.

13. For a discussion of one aspect of pre-Bodenwieser modern dance in Australia see Lynn Fisher, 'Irene Vera Young and the Early Modern Dance in Sydney', *Brolga*, 2, June 1995, pp.7–29.

14. It is not clear whether the front curtain was ever realised, although a design appears in souvenir programs available during the Australian tour by the Monte Carlo Russian Ballet.

15. Walker (1982), p.24.

16. Basil Burdett, 'The Russian Ballet', *The Home*, February 1937, p.41.

17. *Argus* (Melbourne), 25 October 1938, p.18.

18. Press cutting from an unidentified newspaper dated 24 December 1938. Cutting book relating to the de Basil tours, Dennis Wolanski Library of the Performing Arts, Sydney.

19. These and all following statistics relating to Ballets Russes performances and repertoire in Australia are taken from Michelle Potter, The Russian Ballet in Australia 1936–40: sources for Modernism in Australian art, unpublished BA (Hons) thesis, Department of Art History, Australian National University, 1987.

20. Edward H. Pask, *Ballet in Australia: The second act 1940–1980*, Melbourne: Oxford University Press, 1982, p.81.

21. Max Dupain, oral history interview recorded by Michelle Potter in 1990, Esso Performing Arts Collection, National Library of Australia, TRC 2630.

E.O Hoppe Karsavina and Bolm in *L'Oiseau de feu* from *Studies from the Russian Ballet*
National Gallery of Australia

WORKS IN THE EXHIBITION

Drawings and costumes are listed chronologically under the ballets for which they were made. Dates are provided where they are known. The ballets are referred to by their premiere titles, followed by English translations, with separate listings for different productions. Photographs, posters, books, theatre programs and journals in the exhibition are listed on pp. 93–5.

Measurements are given height before width.

Where works are illustrated, page numbers are cited at the end of the relevant entries.

DRAWINGS, COSTUMES
LE PAVILLON D'ARMIDE
(Armida's Pavilion)
Paris premiere: 19 May 1909,
Théâtre du Châtelet, Paris
(first performed Maryinsky Theatre,
St Petersburg, 25 November 1907)
Scenery and costumes: Alexandre Benois
Music: Nicholas Tcherepnine
Choreography: Michel Fokine
Libretto: Alexandre Benois,
after Théophile Gautier's story *Omphale*
Principal dancers: Vera Karalli,
Mikhail Mordkin, Vaslav Nijinsky,
Tamara Karsavina

Alexandre BENOIS
Russia 1870–France 1960
Costume design for Armida's slave 1907
pen, ink, watercolour on paper
31.7 x 14.6 cm
Victoria and Albert Museum, London
(p.27)

Costume design for Armida's slave
pencil, wash, watercolour, silver, bronze and white paint on paper
35.8 x 28.0 cm
St Petersburg State Museum of Theatre and Music

Costume design for Rinaldo 1907
pencil, ink, watercolour, bronze and white paint on paper
35.8 x 28.0 cm
St Petersburg State Museum of Theatre and Music
(p.24)

Costume design for a woman 1907
pencil, watercolour, ink, bronze and white paint on paper
42.0 x 34.0 cm
St Petersburg State Museum of Theatre and Music

Costume for a cavalier 1907
tunic: blue-grey and white cotton, gold lamé, glass beads, gold metallic braid and fringe
inscribed 'Kusov'
St Petersburg State Museum of Theatre and Music

Costume for a woman 1907
bodice and skirt: pink and red silk, cotton lace, gold metallic fringe
St Petersburg State Museum of Theatre and Music

Costume for a spirit of the hours 1909
coat: yellow brushed cotton, silver and black paint, silver metallic braid, gold metallic gauze
tunic with attached waistcoat: gold lamé, silver and black paint, sequins, black silk, gold metallic fringe and sequins
inscribed 'Gairel', 'Chernobaieva'
National Gallery of Australia, Canberra
(p.26)

Costume for a courtier
coat: pink rayon, gold lamé ribbon
tunic: red silk satin, gold lamé, metallic fringe and ribbon, silver metallic braid, cream rayon, cotton lace
inscribed 'Chorand, Barnett, Wygrin'
National Gallery of Australia, Canberra

Costume for a musician
tunic with attached sash and skirt: black brushed cotton, white and orange wool, white, silver and orange paint, imitation jewels (wood, silk velvet, gold metallic braid, sequins and fringe), cream wool sash with silver and orange paint
National Gallery of Australia, Canberra
(p.25)

DANSES POLOVTSIENNES DU PRINCE IGOR
(The Polovtsian Dances from Prince Igor)
Premiere: 19 May 1909,
Théâtre du Châtelet, Paris
Scenery and costumes: Nicholas Roerich
Music: Alexander Borodin (completed and orchestrated by Nikolai Rimsky-Korsakov and Alexander Glazunov)
Choreography: Michel Fokine
Libretto: Alexander Borodin, after a scenario by Vladimir Stasov
Principal dancers: Sophie Fedorova, Adolph Bolm, Elena Smirnova

Nicholas ROERICH
Russia 1874–India 1947
Set design 1909
tempera, body-colour on canvas
58.5 x 84.5 cm
Victoria and Albert Museum, London
(p.6)

Costume for a Polovtsian warrior
c.1910, 1930s
jacket with belt: green and pink striped silk, red, cream and yellow silk ikat, yellow, brown and black dyes
trousers: pink, green, blue and white striped cotton
inscribed 'Burke, N. Semienov'
National Gallery of Australia, Canberra
(p.7)

Costume for a warrior 1910
jacket: green, orange and white silk ikat, metal (worn by Michel Fokine)
St Petersburg State Museum of Theatre and Music

Costume for a Polovtsian girl 1930s
surcoat: natural linen, green and orange paint, brown wool braid, black fur
blouse: yellow cotton, gold metallic braid
trousers: dark purple cotton
inscribed 'Roussova, Sandra'
National Gallery of Australia, Canberra

Cap for a Polovtsian warrior 1930s
orange, yellow, white, green and blue cotton ikat
National Gallery of Australia, Canberra

Cap
khaki wool twill
National Gallery of Australia, Canberra

CLÉOPÂTRE
(Cleopatra)
Paris premiere: 2 June 1909, Théâtre du Châtelet, Paris (originally *Une Nuit d'Egypte* 2 March 1908, St Petersburg)
Scenery and costumes: Léon Bakst
Music: Anton Arensky, Alexander Taneyev, Nikolai Rimsky-Korsakov, Mikhail Glinka, Alexander Glazunov, Modeste Mussorgsky, Nicholas Tcherepnine
Choreography: Michel Fokine
Libretto: Michel Fokine
Principal dancers: Anna Pavlova, Ida Rubinstein, Tamara Karsavina, Vaslav Nijinsky, Michel Fokine, Alexis Bulgakov

Léon BAKST
Belarus 1866–France 1924
Costume for Amoun in Une Nuit d'Egypte
1908
tunic: silk jersey, metallic thread, imitation pearls, metal beads
kilt with apron: silk (worn by Michel Fokine)
St Petersburg State Museum of Theatre and Music

Costume for a Greek 1909
tunic: red silk, pink and red silk appliqué, gold lamé and gold metallic braid
tights: cream silk jersey with grey, red and orange stencilling
inscribed 'Me. de Paoli, Tenor'
National Gallery of Australia, Canberra

Costume for a Jew 1909
coat: green cotton, pink stencilling, tan silk, gold metallic fringe and braid
waistcoat: maroon silk, black stencilling, gold metallic fringe
inscribed 'Kobeleff'
National Gallery of Australia, Canberra
(Canberra only)
(p.31)

Costume for a temple servant 1930s
dress: blue, pink and purple silk faille with silver and gold stencilling, blue silk chiffon and silver metallic braid
collar: pink and purple silk faille, silver metallic braid, gold paint, pink cotton braid
inscribed 'Osato'
National Gallery of Australia, Canberra
(p.28)

CARNAVAL
(Carnival)
Premiere: 20 May 1910, Theater des Westens, Berlin
Scenery and costumes: Léon Bakst
Music: Robert Schumann; orchestrated by Nikolai Rimsky-Korsakov, Anatol Liadov, Alexander Glazunov, Nicholas Tcherepnine
Choreography: Michel Fokine
Libretto: Léon Bakst and Michel Fokine
Principal dancers: Tamara Karsavina, Vaslav Nijinsky, Maria Piltz, Alexis Bulgakov

Léon BAKST
Belarus 1866–France 1924
Costume design for Chiarina 1910
watercolour, pencil on paper on card
27.8 x 21.2 cm
St Petersburg State Museum of Theatre and Music
(p.12)

Costume design for Estrella 1910
watercolour, pencil, heightened with white on paper on card
32.5 x 25.8 cm
St Petersburg State Museum of Theatre and Music

Costume design for Euzebius 1910
watercolour, pencil on paper on card
28.0 x 21.3 cm
St Petersburg State Museum of Theatre and Music

Costume design for Pantalon 1910
watercolour, pencil on paper on card
28.0 x 21.3 cm
St Petersburg State Museum of Theatre and Music

Costume design for a woman in the Noble Waltz 1910
watercolour, pencil on paper on card
36.2 x 24.4 cm
St Petersburg State Museum of Theatre and Music

Costume for Harlequin 1910
blouse: white silk crepe-de-chine
tie: black silk
tights: cream silk jersey with blue and purple stencilling (worn by Michel Fokine)
St Petersburg State Museum of Theatre and Music

Costume for Chiarina 1930s
bodice: off-white acetate, blue and white silk crepe, silk and rayon lace, imitation flowers
skirt: blue silk taffeta, cream cotton tassels
inscribed 'Razoumova'
National Gallery of Australia, Canberra
(p.13)

Costume for Pierrot 1930s?
coat and trousers: cream wool twill, green silk buttons
frilled collar: black cotton organdie
National Gallery of Australia, Canberra

SCHÉHÉRAZADE
Premiere: 4 June 1910, Théâtre National de l'Opéra, Paris
Scenery and costumes: Léon Bakst
Music: Nikolai Rimsky-Korsakov
Choreography: Michel Fokine
Libretto: Léon Bakst and Michel Fokine
Principal dancers: Ida Rubinstein, Vaslav Nijinsky, Alexis Bulgakov, Vassily Kisselov, Enrico Cecchetti

Léon BAKST
Belarus 1866–France 1924
Costume design for an odalisque 1910
gouache, pencil, gold paint, paper on cardboard
29.0 x 19.4 cm
National Gallery of Australia, Canberra
(p.77)

Costume design for Shah Zeman 1910
gouache, pencil, watercolour, gold paint on paper
37.0 x 22.2 cm
National Gallery of Australia, Canberra
(p.76)

Costume for the Chief Eunuch 1910, 1930s
jacket: multi-coloured silk, acetate and rayon, gold metallic braid
trousers: orange silk, yellow silk appliqué
cummerbund: brown silk, gold paint
overskirt: red acetate, white silk appliqué, purple stencilling, gold metallic braid
keys: painted wood
cap: red acetate, blue feathers, gold metallic braid, imitation jewels (glass and metal)
National Gallery of Australia, Canberra
(p.79)

Costume for Shah Shahriar 1930s
coat: burgundy silk velvet, white silk appliqué, gold lamé and metallic braid, painted wooden beads, non-original blue satin sleeves
trousers: blue rayon satin
cap: burgundy silk velvet, blue rayon, imitation jewels (glass and metal)
National Gallery of Australia, Canberra

Costume for Shah Zeman 1930s
coat: green and gold silk brocade, purple silk satin, purple and green silk embroidery, gold lamé and metallic braid, non-original yellow satin
trousers: purple silk satin, gold metallic braid
National Gallery of Australia, Canberra
(pp.74, 75)

Costume for an almée 1930s
one-piece trouser ensemble: green rayon, gold paint, brown cotton velveteen, brown and yellow wool braid
headdress: green rayon, green silk georgette, gold paint
inscribed 'Benks, Markova, Charaska'
National Gallery of Australia, Canberra

Costume for an almée 1930s
one-piece trouser ensemble: pink rayon, pink silk, gold and pink paint, gold metallic braid, green and pink rayon braid, gold gelatin paillettes, glass beads, yellow acetate
headdress: pink and green silk, gold metallic braid
inscribed 'Shea'
National Gallery of Australia, Canberra
(p.78)

Costume for an almée 1930s
one-piece trouser ensemble: purple rayon, blue, pink and orange rayon viscose, gold lamé and metallic braid
inscribed 'Galvin, Kolow'
National Gallery of Australia, Canberra

L'OISEAU DE FEU
(The Firebird)
Premiere: 25 June 1910, Théâtre National de l'Opéra, Paris
Scenery and costumes: Aleksandr Golovin and Léon Bakst
Music: Igor Stravinsky
Choreography: Michel Fokine
Libretto: Michel Fokine, from a Russian folktale
Principal dancers: Tamara Karsavina, Vera Fokina, Michel Fokine, Alexis Bulgakov

Léon BAKST
Belarus 1866–France 1924
Costume design for the Tsarevna 1910
watercolour, bronze paint on paper on card
35.5 x 22.0 cm
St Petersburg State Museum of Theatre and Music
(p.33)

Aleksandr GOLOVIN
Russia 1863–1930
Costume design for an attendant of the Immortal Koshchei 1910
watercolour, pencil, bronze and silver paint on paper
35.5 x 22.0 cm
St Petersburg State Museum of Theatre and Music
(p.35)

Costume design for an attendant of the Immortal Koshchei 1910
watercolour, pencil, white paint on paper
32.7 x 24.8 cm
St Petersburg State Museum of Theatre and Music

Costume design for a woman 1910
watercolour, pencil on paper
36.5 x 24.3 cm
St Petersburg State Museum of Theatre and Music

Costume for a female dancer 1910?
tiered robe: beige cotton with green, pink, blue and black stencilling, white paint
inscribed 'Chand'
National Gallery of Australia, Canberra

Costume for a female dancer 1910?
tiered robe: beige and pink cotton with pink, green, blue and black stencilling, silver metallic and black cotton braid, pink cotton corduroy appliqué
National Gallery of Australia, Canberra

Costume for a female dancer 1910?
tiered robe: beige and pink cotton with pink, green, blue and black stencilling, silver metallic and black cotton braid, pink cotton corduroy appliqué
National Gallery of Australia, Canberra
(Canberra only)

Costume for an attendant of the Immortal Koshchei
tiered and hooped robe: white cotton with gold, black, blue and pink stencilling, metallic brocade ribbon, silver lamé, gold metallic fringe, pink rayon, red paint
belt: blue rayon, white cotton with blue stencilling, black rayon ribbon
inscribed 'Young, Balotine'
National Gallery of Australia, Canberra
(p.34)

NARCISSE
(Narcissus)
Premiere: 26 April 1911, Théâtre de Monte Carlo
Scenery and costumes: Léon Bakst
Music: Nicholas Tcherepnine
Choreography: Michel Fokine
Libretto: Léon Bakst
Principal dancers: Tamara Karsavina, Vaslav Nijinsky, Bronislava Nijinska, Vera Fokina

Léon BAKST
Belarus 1866–France 1924
Costume design for a Bœotian 1911
watercolour, pencil on paper
39.0 x 26.8 cm
St Petersburg State Museum of Theatre and Music

Costume design for a Bœotian youth 1911
watercolour on paper
40.0 x 27.5 cm
St Petersburg State Museum of Theatre and Music
(p.60)

Costume design for two Bœotian girls 1911
watercolour on paper
40.5 x 27.5 cm
St Petersburg State Museum of Theatre and Music

Costume for a Bœotian youth 1911
robe: yellow wool with orange, brown, green and blue stencilling, gold metallic braid
inscribed 'G.Varzhinski'
National Gallery of Australia, Canberra
(p.61)

Costume for a Bœotian girl 1911
robe: blue wool, cream wool appliqué with green and blue stencilling, gold metallic braid, metal buttons
inscribed 'Doreen, Kamerova'
National Gallery of Australia, Canberra
(p.61)

Cloak for Echo 1911
dark blue wool, gold stencilling
National Gallery of Australia, Canberra

SADKO
Premiere: 6 June 1911,
Théâtre du Châtelet, Paris
Scenery and costumes: Boris Anisfeld
and Léon Bakst
Music: Nikolai Rimsky-Korsakov
Choreography: Michel Fokine
Libretto: Nikolai Rimsky-Korsakov
and Vladimir Belsky
Principal dancers: Lubov Tchernicheva,
Vera Nemchinova, Leon Woizikovsky

Boris ANISFELD
Russia 1879–1973
Costume design for the Golden Fish 1911
watercolour, gouache, bronze paint on paper
45.9 x 26.5 cm
St Petersburg State Museum of Theatre and Music
(p.19)

Costume design for the Mermaid 1911
watercolour, gouache, pencil on paper
47.0 x 28.6 cm
St Petersburg State Museum of Theatre and Music
(p.19)

Costume design for the Sea Queen 1911
watercolour, gouache, pencil on paper
46.0 x 20.0 cm
St Petersburg State Museum of Theatre and Music

Costume design for the Sea Queen 1911
watercolour, gouache, pencil on paper
45.8 x 20.0 cm
St Petersburg State Museum of Theatre and Music

Costume design for Volkhova 1911
pencil, watercolour, gouache on paper on card
46.0 x 28.8 cm
St Petersburg State Museum of Theatre and Music

PETROUCHKA
(Petrushka)
Premiere: 13 June 1911,
Théâtre du Châtelet, Paris
Scenery and costumes: Alexandre Benois
Music: Igor Stravinsky
Choreography: Michel Fokine
Libretto: Igor Stravinsky
and Alexandre Benois
Principal dancers: Tamara Karsavina,
Vaslav Nijinsky, Alexander Orlov,
Enrico Cecchetti

Alexandre BENOIS
Russia 1870–France 1960
Costume design for a coachman 1911
watercolour, gouache on paper
31.0 x 23.2 cm
St Petersburg State Museum of Theatre and Music

Costume design for a devil *c.*1920
brush and ink, pen and ink, watercolour,
pencil on paper
31.8 x 21.4 cm
National Gallery of Australia, Canberra

Costume design for a merchant *c.*1920
watercolour, pen and ink, pencil on paper
32.0 x 21.2 cm
National Gallery of Australia, Canberra

Costume design for a peasant woman
*c.*1920
watercolour, pen and ink, pencil on paper
31.6 x 23.0 cm
National Gallery of Australia, Canberra
(p.37)

Costume design for a reveller in a pig mask
*c.*1920
watercolour, pen and ink, pencil on paper
31.0 x 23.6 cm
National Gallery of Australia, Canberra
(p.37)

Set design for the Moor's room *c.*1920
pen and ink, gouache, watercolour,
pen and green ink on paper
14.2 x 21.8 cm
National Gallery of Australia, Canberra
(p.36)

Backdrop and wings
cotton, distemper, dyes, charcoal, metal
National Gallery of Australia, Canberra

Costume for the Ballerina 1918
jacket, blouse, skirt and trousers: silk, wool,
velvet, lace, imitation fur
(worn by Tamara Karsavina)
St Petersburg State Museum of Theatre and Music

Costume for Petrouchka
tunic: white cotton, red and blue silk satin
ribbon, pink satin cuffs, black cotton lace
trousers: pink silk satin, yellow silk-cotton
Skinner's satin
boots: blue kid
inscribed 'Nijinski'
National Gallery of Australia, Canberra
(p.38)

LE DIEU BLEU
(The Blue God)
Premiere: 13 May 1912,
Théâtre du Châtelet, Paris
Scenery and costumes: Léon Bakst
Music: Reynaldo Hahn
Choreography: Michel Fokine
Libretto: Jean Cocteau
and Federigo de Madrazo
Principal dancers: Tamara Karsavina,
Vaslav Nijinsky, Lydia Nelidova,
Max Frohman

Léon BAKST
Belarus 1866–France 1924
Costume design for the Sacrificial Bearer 1911
gouache, pencil, gold paint
28.4 x 23.0 cm
National Gallery of Australia, Canberra

Set design 1911
charcoal, watercolour, gouache on paper
55.8 x 78.0 cm
Bequest of R. Lemasle 1974, Musée national
d'art moderne — Centre de création
industrielle, Centre Georges Pompidou, Paris
(p.42)

Costume design for the Sacred Dance 1912
watercolour, pencil, gold paint on paper
43.0 x 28.0 cm
Purchased 1982, Musée national d'art
moderne — Centre de création industrielle,
Centre Georges Pompidou, Paris
(p.41)

Costume for the Blue God 1912
tunic: cream silk moiré faille, purple and
green printed silk, pink, blue and cream silk
satin, green silk velvet ribbon, coloured silk
braid, metal and silk thread embroidery,
gold metal studs, gelatin 'mother-of-pearl'
discs
crown: gold metallic gauze, silk thread
embroidery, gelatin sequins, metal studs,
gold and green paint, gold metallic braid
and paillettes
inscribed 'Nijinsky'
National Gallery of Australia, Canberra
(p.43)

Three headdresses from costumes for the
Little Gods 1912
papier maché, gold metallic gauze, braid,
cord and medallions
Theatre Museum, Victoria and Albert
Museum, London

THAMAR

Premiere: 20 May 1912,
Théâtre du Châtelet, Paris
Scenery and costumes: Léon Bakst
Music: Mily Alexeyevich Balakirev
Choreography: Michel Fokine
Libretto: Léon Bakst
Principal dancers: Tamara Karsavina,
Adolph Bolm

Léon BAKST
Belarus 1866–France 1924
Costume for Queen Thamar 1930s
dress: light purple acetate, silver metallic
braid, cream silk satin, blue silk, metal
squares
vest: silver lamé, blue silk, metallic braid,
metal squares
overskirt: silver lamé and metallic braid,
cream silk, blue silk embroidery, imitation
jewels (metal and glass)
veil: cream silk, silver and blue paint
crown: silver metallic braid, light purple
acetate, cream acetate, metal squares
National Gallery of Australia, Canberra
(pp.9, 10)

Costume for a guard
coat: pink and green silk satin, blue, yellow
and green silk, metallic ribbon, silk with
black stencilling, painted wood
trousers: green silk, cream silk appliqué,
stencilled silver metallic braid, green
silk ribbon
belt: metallic ribbon, imitation jewels
(glass, metal)
cap: black wool-cotton imitation Persian
lamb, black silk satin, metallic braid
inscribed 'Vladim, Maligine, Burns,
Daman, Stephens'
National Gallery of Australia, Canberra
(p.9)

L'APRES-MIDI D'UN FAUNE
(The Afternoon of a Faun)
Premiere: 29 May 1912,
Théâtre du Châtelet, Paris
Scenery and costumes: Léon Bakst
Music: Claude Debussy
Choreography: Vaslav Nijinsky
Libretto: Vaslav Nijinsky, after a poem
by Stephane Mallarmé
Principal dancers: Vaslav Nijinsky,
Lydia Nelidova

Léon BAKST
Belarus 1866–France 1924
Set design 1912
gouache on paper
75.0 x 105.0 cm
Purchased 1932, Musée national d'art
moderne — Centre de création industrielle,
Centre Georges Pompidou, Paris
(p.63)

Costume for a nymph 1930s
dress: beige silk chiffon with blue stencilling,
gold lamé ribbon and underskirt
inscribed 'Goloven, Deni'
National Gallery of Australia, Canberra
(p.62)

Costume for a nymph 1930s
dress: beige silk chiffon with green and blue
stencilling, gold lamé ribbon and underskirt
inscribed 'Osato, Olrich, Couprina'
National Gallery of Australia, Canberra
(p.62)

Costume for a nymph 1930s
dress: beige silk chiffon with red and green
stencilling, gold lamé ribbon and underskirt
inscribed 'Milton, Stepanova, Lvova'
National Gallery of Australia, Canberra
(p.62)

DAPHNIS ET CHLOÉ
(Daphnis and Chloë)
Premiere: 8 June 1912,
Théâtre du Châtelet, Paris
Scenery and costumes: Léon Bakst
Music: Maurice Ravel
Choreography: Michel Fokine
Libretto: Michel Fokine,
based on a poem by Longus
Principal dancers: Tamara Karsavina,
Vaslav Nijinsky, Adolph Bolm

Léon BAKST
Russia 1866–France 1924
Costume for a brigand 1912
tunic and belt: blue and white wool with
white, orange and red stencilling
shorts: blue and white wool with red
stencilling
cloak: blue and cream wool with maroon
and black stencilling, maroon, black and
cream wool appliqué, cream cotton
inscribed 'Kostetski'
National Gallery of Australia, Canberra
(p.45)

Costume for a brigand 1912
tunic: purple, cream and black wool with
black and white stencilling
belt: cream cotton with black stencilling
inscribed 'Zvirev, Kegler'
National Gallery of Australia, Canberra
(p.44)

Costume for a brigand 1912
tunic and belt: blue wool with white
stencilling, orange and white wool
inscribed 'Loboika, Kovalski'
National Gallery of Australia, Canberra

Costume for a brigand 1912
tunic, shorts and belt: yellow, cream and
black wool with green and black stencilling
inscribed 'Zyvrev, Kremnev'
National Gallery of Australia, Canberra
(p.44)

Cloak for a brigand 1912
blue grey cotton with black stencilling, red
and brown wool appliqué
National Gallery of Australia, Canberra

Cloak for a brigand 1912
yellow (mustard) wool with black and brown
stencilling, white wool appliqué
National Gallery of Australia, Canberra

Three hats from costumes for brigands 1912
headscarf: red wool with white and orange
stencilling
hood: brown and black wool felt, brown
cotton canvas and leather
headdress: brown wool flannel, black cloth
appliqué, carmine vermilion cloth with
green, white and black stencilling
inscribed 'Lobojko, Kostekoi, Gavrilov'
Theatre Museum, Victoria and Albert
Museum, London

LE SACRE DU PRINTEMPS
(The Rite of Spring)
Premiere: 29 May 1913,
Théâtre des Champs-Elysée, Paris
Scenery and costumes: Nicholas Roerich
Music: Igor Stravinsky
Choreography: Vaslav Nijinsky
Libretto: Igor Stravinsky and
Nicholas Roerich
Principal dancers: Marie Piltz,
Constantin Woronzov

Nicholas ROERICH
Russia 1874–India 1947
Costume design for a maiden 1912
pencil, gouache, watercolour, bronze paint
on cardboard
24.3 x 15.2 cm
A.A. Bakhrushin State Central Theatre
Museum, Moscow
(p.14)

Costume design for a youth 1912
pencil, watercolour, bronze and silver paint
on cardboard
25.1 x 15.8 cm
A.A. Bakhrushin State Central Theatre
Museum, Moscow
(p.14)

Costume for a maiden 1913
robe: off-white and red wool, orange cotton,
both with yellow, brown, green, red, grey,
blue and orange stencilling
belt: leather, metal 'horse' amulet
slippers: white suede, blue and red paint
inscribed 'Schegolikha, Fedorov'
Theatre Museum, Victoria and Albert
Museum, London
(p.15)

Costume for a man 1913
robe: off-white flannelette, orange cotton,
both with red, brown, pink, blue and purple
stencilling
belt: leather, stamped metal
discs, painted wooden dagger
cap: white cotton brown fur, red, purple,
pink and brown paint
inscribed 'Fedorov, Statkiewia, Vulrikii'
Theatre Museum, Victoria and Albert
Museum, London

LE COQ D'OR
(The Golden Cockerel)
Premiere: 24 May 1914, Théâtre National
de l'Opéra, Paris
Scenery and costumes: Natalia
Goncharova
Music: Nikolai Rimsky-Korsakov
Choreography: Michel Fokine
Libretto: Vladimir Belsky after Aleksandr
Pushkin, revised by Alexandre Benois
Principal dancers: Tamara Karsavina,
Alexis Bulgakov, Enrico Cecchetti

Natalia GONCHAROVA
Russia 1881–France 1962
Costume design for a peasant woman 1914
gouache and pencil on cardboard
37.8 x 26.8 cm
National Gallery of Australia, Canberra
(p.47)

Set design for Act III 1914
watercolour, gouache, collage on cardboard
63.5 x 96.3 cm
A.A. Bakhrushin State Central Theatre
Museum, Moscow
(p.48)

Costume design for a male Russian peasant
watercolour, body-colour on paper
38.0 x 27.0 cm
Victoria and Albert Museum, London

***Costume design for a Russian peasant
with a flask of vodka***
watercolour, body-colour on paper
38.0 x 26.5 cm
Victoria and Albert Museum, London

SADKO
Premiere: 9 October 1916, Manhattan
Opera House, New York
Scenery and costumes: Natalia Goncharova
(with 1911 set by Boris Anisfeld)
Music: Nikolai Rimsky-Korsakov
Choreography: Adolph Bolm
Libretto: Nikolai Rimsky-Korsakov
and Vladimir Belsky
Principal dancers: Adolph Bolm,
Miss Doris, Jean Jazwinsky

Natalia GONCHAROVA
Russia 1881–France 1962
Costume design for a seahorse 1916
pencil, watercolour, body-colour with
tin-foil
21.5 x 15.0 cm
Victoria and Albert Museum, London
(p.19)

Costume for a seahorse 1916
headdress: yellow, brown and white
silk-cotton satin, gold lamé and ribbon,
brown cotton piping, red ribbon, red dye
cape: yellow, brown and cream silk-cotton
satin, gold lamé and metallic braid, red dye
(non-original restoration fabrics)
blouse and trousers: yellow and brown
silk-cotton satin, red dye
inscribed 'Mr Novak, Kavezk, Kawecki'
National Gallery of Australia, Canberra
(p.18)

CLÉOPÂTRE
(Cleopatra)
Premiere: 5 September 1918, Coliseum
Theatre, London.
Revival of 1909 production with
additional set and costumes by Robert
and Sonia Delaunay
Principal dancers: Léonide Massine,
Lubov Tchernicheva, Lydia Sokolova

Sonia DELAUNAY
Ukraine 1885–France 1979
Costume for Amoun 1918–1930s
yoke and shoulder straps: black cotton
velveteen, purple wool, gold metallic braid
kilt with apron: purple cotton, gold leather,
black, red and orange silk velvet, green silk,
gold metallic braid
National Gallery of Australia, Canberra

Costume for a slave girl 1918–1930s
dress: orange and blue wool, orange viscose-
cotton satin, gold lamé, metallic fringe,
ribbon, braid and paint
collar: rayon, cotton, gold metallic braid
National Gallery of Australia, Canberra

Costume for a slave girl 1918–1930s
dress: orange and blue wool, orange viscose-cotton satin, gold lamé, metallic braid, ribbon and paint
inscribed 'Volokova'
Gift of Elaine Lustig Cohen in memory of Michael Lloyd 1997
National Gallery of Australia, Canberra
(p.30)

LA BOUTIQUE FANTASQUE
(The Magical Toyshop)
Premiere: 5 June 1919, Alhambra Theatre, London
Scenery and costumes: André Derain
Music: Gioacchino Rossini, arranged and orchestrated by Ottorino Respighi
Choreography: Léonide Massine
Libretto: Serge Diaghilev, Léonide Massine, Serge Grigoriev, André Derain, after *Puppenfee* (The Fairy Doll) by Josef Bayer
Principal dancers: Lydia Lopokova, Léonide Massine, Enrico Cecchetti, Josephine Cechetti, Serge Grigoriev, Lydia Sokolova, Léon Woizikovsky, Nicholas Zverev, Vera Clark, Nicholas Kremnev

André DERAIN
France 1880–1954
Costume design for the Can-Can Dancer
1918–19
watercolour, pen and ink, pencil on paper
31.6 x 24.8 cm
National Gallery of Australia, Canberra

Costume for the male Poodle 1919
bodysuit: white cotton jersey, imitation fur (white flax, mohair and cotton)
mask with snout: wool felt, linoleum, black paint
National Gallery of Australia, Canberra
(Canberra only)

LE CHANT DU ROSSIGNOL
(The Song of the Nightingale)
Premiere: 2 February 1920, Théâtre National de l'Opéra, Paris
Scenery and costumes: Henri Matisse
Music: Igor Stravinsky
Choreography: Léonide Massine
Libretto: after the story by Hans Christian Andersen
Principal dancers: Tamara Karsavina, Lydia Sokolova, Serge Grigoriev, Stanislas Idzikovsky

Henri MATISSE
France 1869–1954
Costume for a chamberlain 1920
robe: cream silk satin, orange, black and grey ink, gold lamé appliqué, gold and black silk ribbon
National Gallery of Australia, Canberra
(Canberra only)
(p.53)

Costume for a mandarin 1920
robe: yellow silk satin, gold lamé, black ink
National Gallery of Australia, Canberra
(p.52)

Costume for a mourner 1920
coat with attached hood: cream cotton-wool felt, navy silk-cotton velvet appliqué, black ink
National Gallery of Australia, Canberra
(p.50)

Costume for a court lady 1920
tunic: pale pink silk satin, embroidered gold lamé, graphite, black silk velvet
inscribed, 'Estomina'
National Gallery of Australia, Canberra

Costume for a court lady 1920
tunic: pale pink silk satin, embroidered gold lamé, graphite, black silk velvet
inscribed, 'Clementovich'
National Gallery of Australia, Canberra
(Perth only)

LE ASTUZIE FEMMINILI
(Woman's Wiles)
Premiere: 27 May 1920, Théâtre National de l'Opéra, Paris
Scenery and costumes: José Maria Sert
Music: Domenico Cimarosa, orchestrated by Ottorino Respighi
Choreography: Léonide Massine
Libretto: Giuseppe Palomba
Principal dancers: Lubov Tchernicheva, Vera Nemchinova, Tamara Karsavina, Zygmund Novak, Lydia Sokolova, Léon Woizikovsky, Stanislav Idzikovsky

José Maria SERT
Spain 1874–1945 also worked in France
Costume for Dr Romualdo 1920
coat with false waistcoat and breeches: beige cotton velveteen, black and orange paint, black silk velvet, grey cotton velveteen, metal buttons
inscribed 'Mr Cappellali'
National Gallery of Australia, Canberra

Hat 1920
burgundy silk-cotton velvet, silk and gold metallic braid
National Gallery of Australia, Canberra

Top hat from a costume for Giampaolo
1920
black cotton velveteen, cream silk appliqué, coloured cotton braid
National Gallery of Australia, Canberra

CHOUT
(The Buffoon)
Premiere: 17 May 1921, Théâtre de la Gaîté-Lyrique, Paris
Scenery and costumes: Michel Larionov
Music: Serge Prokofiev
Choreography: Michel Larionov and Thadée Slavinsky
Libretto: Serge Diaghilev
Principal dancers: Thadée Slavinsky, Lydia Sokolova, Jean Jazvinsky, Catherine Devillier

Michel LARIONOV
Moldova 1881–France 1964
Costume design for the Chief Clown 1915
watercolour, body-colour on paper
67.5 x 47.7 cm
Victoria and Albert Museum, London
(p.71)

Costume design for the Merchant 1915
gouache, pencil
69.5 x 38.0 cm
Victoria and Albert Museum, London
(p.71)

Set design for the Merchant's garden 1921
watercolour
47.3 x 60.3 cm
Österreichisches Theatermuseum, Vienna
(p.71)

Blouse from costume for a bridesmaid 1921
bodice: orange cotton sateen, brown, red,
maroon and green cotton sateen appliqué,
blue, red and green paint, brown cotton
sateen buttons
National Gallery of Australia, Canberra
(p.73)

Costume for a buffoon's wife 1921
blouse: cotton with pink and orange dyes
apron with attached 'wings': painted
buckram and cotton with cane support
trousers: white brushed cotton, pink and
purple silk, orange cotton, blue and black
cotton appliqué
collar: brown cotton sateen, white brushed
cotton, yellow cotton piping
inscribed 'Hantzka?, Haviska, Plotankova'
National Gallery of Australia, Canberra
(p.70)

Costume for a soldier 1921
jacket: blue, white, tan, pink and black
brushed cotton, red leatherette, cotton
buckram, yellow cotton, red paint
breeches: blue, white, black and tan brushed
cotton, red leatherette, yellow and grey
cotton
mask with hat: buckram, cotton sateen, paint
inscribed 'Pavlov'
National Gallery of Australia, Canberra
(Canberra only)
(p.72)

THE SLEEPING PRINCESS

Premiere: 2 November 1921, Alhambra,
London
Scenery and costumes: Léon Bakst
Music: Pyotr Il'yich Tchaikovsky and
Igor Stravinsky
Choreography: Marius Petipa (reproduced
by Nicholas Sergeyev), Bronislava Nijinska
Libretto: Marius Petipa and
I. Vsevolozhsky, after Charles Perrault
Principal dancers: Olga Spessivtseva,
Lydia Lopokova, Carlotta Brianza,
Lubov Tchernicheva, Bronislava Nijinska,
Pierre Vladimirov, Anatole Vilzak,
Stanislav Idzikovsky, Leon Woizikovsky,
Léonard Treer, Vera Sudeikina,
Jean Jazvinsky

Léon BAKST
Belarus 1866–France 1924
Costume design for Columbine 1921
watercolour, body-colour, gold paint, pencil
on paper
29.2 x 22.5 cm
Victoria and Albert Museum, London

Costume design for the Queen and her page
1921
watercolour, pencil, gold and silver paint
on paper on card
29.2 x 44.6 cm
National Gallery of Australia, Canberra
(p.68)

Costume for the Bluebird 1921
doublet: royal and pale blue silk satin,
imitation jewels (plastic), cream cotton
jersey, pink silk crepe, gold metallic braid
and paint
cap: royal blue silk satin, imitation jewels
(plastic), gold metallic braid
National Gallery of Australia, Canberra
(p.69)

Costume for a lady-in-waiting 1921
ballgown: orange, green and cream silk
satin, white silk chiffon, green silk velvet,
cream silk, blue silk satin ribbon, gold
metallic braid and fringe, green and silver
ink, swansdown fur, imitation jewels (wood,
paint, metal, glass, gelatin discs, lacquer)
inscribed 'A.Rosenski'
National Gallery of Australia, Canberra
(p.67)

Costume for the English Prince 1921
coat: pink velvet with gold paint stencilling,
red repp appliqué, white silk, gold metallic
braid and brass studs
waistcoat: red repp, white satin,
gold metallic embroidery and fringe
Theatre Museum, Victoria and Albert
Museum, London
(p.66)

LE MARIAGE DE LA BELLE AU BOIS DORMANT
(Aurora's Wedding)
Premiere: 18 May 1922, Théâtre National
de l'Opéra, Paris
Scenery and costumes: Alexandre Benois
(*Le Pavillon d'Armide*), new costumes
by Natalia Goncharova
Music: Pyotr Il'yich Tchaikovsky
Choreography: after Marius Petipa
Libretto: Marius Petipa
and I. Vsevolozhsky, after Charles
Perrault's fairytale
Principal dancers: Vera Trefilova,
Pierre Vladimirov, Nina Oghinska,
Stanislav Idzikovsky

Natalia GONCHAROVA
Russia 1881–France 1962
Costume for an Ivan 1930s
tunic: pale green silk satin, silk-cotton
grosgrain, pink and blue silk appliqué,
gold metallic braid
trousers: blue acetate satin
inscribed 'Joukovsky, Rueda, Klimof,
Harvey, Orskov'
National Gallery of Australia, Canberra
(p.68)

CIMAROSIANA

Premiere: 8 January 1924,
Théâtre de Monte Carlo
Scenery and costumes: José Maria Sert
Music: orchestrated by Ottorino Respighi
(after Domenico Cimarosa)
Choreography: Léonide Massine
Libretto: Guiseppi Palomba
Principal dancers: Vera Nemchinova,
Lubov Tchernicheva, Lydia Sokolova,
Stanislav Idzikovsky, Leon Woizikowsky,
Anatole Vilzak, Alice Nikitina,
Ninette de Valois, Constantin Tcherkas,
Serge Lifar, Alexandra Danilova,
Léonide Massine

José Maria SERT
Spain 1876–1945 also worked in France
**Tall cap from a costume for the Military
corps** 1924
black felt, pink cotton, feather plume,
cream cotton braid and tassel
National Gallery of Australia, Canberra

ZÉPHIRE ET FLORE
(Zephyr and Flora)
Premiere: 28 April 1925,
Théâtre de Monte Carlo
Scenery and costumes: Georges Braque
Music: Vladimir Dukelsky
Choreography: Léonide Massine
Libretto: Boris Kochno
Principal dancers: Alice Nikitina,
Anton Dolin, Serge Lifar

Georges BRAQUE
France 1882–1963
Helmet from costume for Boreas 1925
papier maché, gold paint,
ostrich feathers
National Gallery of Australia, Canberra

Costume for Zephyr 1925
overskirt: gold lamé, paper flowers, silver
paint, tinsel and wire
cap: textured gold lamé
National Gallery of Australia, Canberra

Headdress from costume for a muse 1925
gold lamé, metallic braid and thread, black
silk discs, gold metallic braid, glass beads,
silver paint
National Gallery of Australia, Canberra

Oliver MESSEL
Great Britain 1904–West Indies 1978
Mask from costume for a muse 1925
papier maché, gold and black paint
inscribed 'Tchernicheva'
National Gallery of Australia, Canberra

L'OISEAU DE FEU
(The Firebird)
Premiere: 25 November 1926,
Lyceum Theatre, London
Scenery and costumes: Natalia
Goncharova
Music: Igor Stravinsky
Choreography: Michel Fokine
Libretto: Michel Fokine, from a Russian
folktale
Principal dancers: Lydia Lopokova,
Lubov Tchernicheva, Serge Lifar,
George Balanchine

Natalia GONCHAROVA
Russia 1881–France 1962
Costume for an attendant to Koshchei 1926
robe: rust wool, gold leatherette, white
cotton appliqué, glass beads, black cotton
braid, gold metallic brocade ribbon,
light red cotton
National Gallery of Australia, Canberra
(Canberra only)

ODE
Premiere: 6 June 1928, Théâtre Sarah
Bernhardt, Paris
Scenery and costumes: Pavel Tchelitchev
and Pierre Charbonnier
Music: Nikolai Nabokov
Choreography: Léonide Massine
Libretto: Boris Kochno after *Spiritual Odes*
by Mikhail Lomonosov
Principal dancers: Ira Beliamina,
Serge Lifar, Felia Doubrovska,
Alice Nikitina, Léonide Massine,
Nicolas Efimov, Constantin Tcherkass

Pavel TCHELITCHEV
Russia 1898–Italy 1957
Costume for a constellation 1928
leotard and tights: blue cotton jersey,
zinc and barium paint
mask: wire mesh
National Gallery of Australia, Canberra
(p.23)

Costume for a star 1928
ballgown: iridescent grey rayon-cotton,
black cotton, bakelite mirror
mask: wire mesh
National Gallery of Australia, Canberra
(p.22)

LE BAL
(The Ball)
Premiere: 7 May 1929,
Théâtre de Monte Carlo
Scenery and costumes: Giorgio de Chirico
Music: Vittorio Rieti
Choreography: George Balanchine
Libretto: Boris Kochno, after a novel
by Count Vladimir Sollogub
Principal dancers: Alexandra Danilova,
Anton Dolin, André Bobrow, Serge Lifar,
Eugenia Lipovska, Felia Dubrovska,
Leon Woizikovsky, George Balanchine

Giorgio DE CHIRICO
Greece 1888–Italy 1978
Costume for a male guest 1929
jacket: light brown and green wool, cream
cotton grosgrain, black rayon ribbon, black
wool thread embroidery, black ink
dickey: cream cotton grosgrain, black wool
embroidery and ribbon
trousers: cream wool, black dye
inscribed 'Borovski'
National Gallery of Australia, Canberra
(p.16)

Jacket for the Young Man 1935?
jacket with epaulettes: cream and burgundy
wool flannel, burgundy, cream, orange and
green wool appliqué, black rayon braid
National Gallery of Australia, Canberra
(p.17)

LES PRÉSAGES
(Destiny)
Premiere: 13 April 1933,
Théâtre de Monte Carlo
Scenery and costumes: André Masson
Music: Pyotr Il'yich Tchaikovsky,
Fifth Symphony in E minor
Choreography: Léonide Massine
Libretto: Léonide Massine
Principal dancers: Nina Verchinina,
Irina Baronova, Tatiana Riabouchinska,
David Lichine, Leon Woizikowsky

André MASSON
France 1896–1987
Study for the stage curtain 1932
pastel on paper
40.5 x 47.5 cm
Fondation André Masson, Paris

Costume design for Fate 1933
charcoal, pastel on paper
59.0 x 47.0 cm
Fondation André Masson, Paris
(p.82)

Costume design for the Spring costumes 1933
pastel on paper
48.0 x 63.0 cm
Fondation André Masson, Paris

Costume design for two figures 1933
pastel on paper
50.0 x 65.0 cm
Fondation André Masson, Paris

Design for the set and wings 1933
pastel on paper
41.5 x 50.0 cm
Fondation André Masson, Paris
(p.82)

Study for the final scene 1933
pastel on paper
40.0 x 45.0 cm
Fondation André Masson, Paris

Study for the stage curtain 1933
pastel on paper
37.0 x 48.0 cm
Fondation André Masson, Paris

Costumes for two men from Scene 1 1933
two jackets: burgundy and green wool
inscribed 'P.Sota, Chabelevsky'
National Gallery of Australia, Canberra
(p.81)

Costume for a woman from Scene 1 1933
dress: purple rayon, dark purple velvet
appliqué
inscribed 'Voronova, Charaska, Bentley'
National Gallery of Australia, Canberra

Costumes for two women from Scene 2 1933
two dresses: grey rayon, black rayon braid,
red silk velvet appliqué and embroidery
inscribed 'Constantine, Evans, June King,
Wassipeva, Oukow'
National Gallery of Australia, Canberra
(p.80)

LE COQ D'OR
(The Golden Cockerel)
Premiere: 23 September 1937,
Covent Garden, London
Scenery and costumes: Natalia Goncharova
Music: Nikolai Rimsky-Korsakov, adapted
by Nicholas Tcherepnine
Choreography: Michel Fokine
Libretto: Vladimir Belsky, after a story
by Aleksandr Pushkin, revised by
Alexandre Benois
Principal dancers: Tatiana Riabouchinska,
Irina Baronova, Marc Platoff, H. Algeranoff

Natalia GONCHAROVA
Russia 1881–France 1962
Costume for King Dodon 1937
robe: pink silk grosgrain, burgundy and red
cotton velveteen, yellow wool, gold lamé,
gold metallic braid
mantle (shown separately): red cotton
velveteen, cream silk and gold lamé, collar
trimmed with braid of real gold, lining of
white brushed cotton and ermine tails
National Gallery of Australia, Canberra
(pp.48, 49)

Costume for a peasant woman 1937
pinafore: orange cotton, blue, white, green,
orange and red cotton appliqué, orange and
red cotton braid, yellow wool ribbon
blouse: white linen, orange cotton appliqué,
red cotton braid
inscribed 'Karinska, Galwan, Francis'
National Gallery of Australia, Canberra
(p.46)

ICARE
(Icarus)
Premiere: 16 February 1940,
Theatre Royal, Sydney
Scenery and costumes: Sidney Nolan
Music: rhythms by Serge Lifar, orchestrated
by Antal Dorati
Choreography: Serge Lifar
Libretto: Serge Lifar, adapted from the
Greek legend
Principal dancers: Serge Lifar,
Dimitri Rostoff

Sidney NOLAN
Australia 1917–Great Britain 1992
Set design 1940
gouache, ink, pencil, collage on card
37.8 x 41.2 cm
National Gallery of Australia, Canberra
(p.83)

LA LUTTE ETERNELLE
(The Eternal Struggle)
Premiere: 29 July 1940,
Theatre Royal, Sydney
Scenery and costumes: Kathleen
and Florence Martin
Music: Robert Schumann, arranged
by Antal Dorati
Choreography: Igor Schwezov
Libretto: Igor Schwezov
Principal dancers: George Skibine,
Marina Svetlova, Sono Osato

Florence MARTIN
Australia 1908–1984
also worked in the United States
and Europe 1942–1972
Costume design for Obsessions 1940
gouache, pencil on card
37.9 x 27.8 cm
National Gallery of Australia, Canberra

PHOTOGRAPHS, POSTERS, BOOKS

N. ALEKSANDROV
Russia
The Diaghilev company in rehearsal
c.1909–1910
gelatin silver photograph
22.2 x 29.0 cm
St Petersburg State Museum of Theatre and Music

**The Diaghilev company in rehearsal
for** Le Carnaval c.1909–1910
gelatin silver photograph
22.2 x 29.0 cm
St Petersburg State Museum of Theatre and Music

George BARBIER
France 1882–1932
**Vaslav Nijinsky as the Golden Slave and Ida
Rubinstein as Zobeide in** Schéhérazade from
Designs on the dances of Vaslav Nijinsky
(London: C.W. Beaumont, 1913)
lineblock, watercolour
edition 30/400
National Gallery of Australia Research Library,
Canberra
(p.56)

Vene BECK
Australia 1893–?
Scene from Icare 1940
gelatin silver photograph
16.6 x 24.6 cm
Gift of Mrs Haydn Beck and her daughter
Mrs Norma Johnstone 1982
National Gallery of Australia, Canberra

Auguste BERT (see also HOPPE)
France
Nijinsky as the Bluebird in Le Festin 1909
gelatin silver photograph on board,
autographed by Vaslav Nijinsky
21.0 x 13.4; 35.0 x 29.0 cm
National Gallery of Australia, Canberra

Jean COCTEAU
France 1889–1963
**Poster of Tamara Karsavina
in** Le Spectre de la rose 1911
colour lithograph
201.0 x 132.0 cm
St Petersburg State Museum of Theatre and Music

Poster of Vaslav Nijinsky in Le Spectre
de la rose 1911
colour lithograph
197.2 x 123.0 cm
National Gallery of Australia, Canberra
(p.59)

DOVER STREET STUDIOS, London

ELLIOT & FRY, London
Great Britain est.1863–1963
Vaslav Nijinsky as Petrouchka c.1913
gelatin silver photograph
20.0 x 15.1 cm
National Gallery of Australia, Canberra
(p.39)

Vaslav Nijinsky as Petrouchka c.1913
gelatin silver photograph
14.8 x 11.2 cm
Gift of Mrs Diana Woollard 1980
National Gallery of Australia, Canberra

Portrait of Vaslav Nijinsky c.1913
gelatin silver photograph
14.4 x 10.7 cm
National Gallery of Australia, Canberra

Max DUPAIN
Australia 1911–1992
Portrait of Col. W. de Basil 1940
gelatin silver photograph
47.1 x 34.9 cm
National Gallery of Australia, Canberra

Karl FISHER
Russia 1856–1917
St Petersburg Imperial Theatres' dressmaking studio for women's costumes c.1890
gelatin silver photograph
32.2 x 41.2 cm
St Petersburg State Museum of Theatre and Music

Anna Pavlova and Vaslav Nijinsky as Armida and slave in Le Pavillon d'Armide 1908
gelatin silver photograph
13.6 x 8.7 cm
St Petersburg State Museum of Theatre and Music
(p.27)

Vaslav Nijinsky as the slave in Le Pavillon d' Armide 1908
gelatin silver photograph
13.8 x 8.8 cm
St Petersburg State Museum of Theatre and Music

FLEET STREET photographers, London
Great Britain
Tamara Karsavina as Zobeide in Schéhérazade 1911
gelatin silver photograph
23.5 x 17.3 cm
St Petersburg State Museum of Theatre and Music

E.O. HOPPE
Germany 1878–Great Britain 1972
with **Auguste BERT**
France
Studies from the Russian Ballet
(London: Fine Arts Society, 1913)
portfolio of 15 rotogravure photographs
National Gallery of Australia

L'Oiseau de feu – Madame Thamar Karsavina
18.4 x 15.4 cm
(p.32)

L'Oiseau de feu – Madame Thamar Karsavina
20.6 x 11.4 cm

L'Oiseau de feu – Madame Thamar Karsavina and M. Adolph Bolm
20.4 x 15.4 cm

L'Oiseau de feu – Monsieur Adolph Bolm
20.4 x 15.4 cm

Thamar – Monsieur Adolph Bolm
20.4 x 15.4 cm

Thamar – Madame Thamar Karsavina and M. Adolph Bolm
20.4 x 15.4 cm
(p.11)

Le Spectre de la Rose – Madame Thamar Karsavina
20.4 x 14.6 cm

(Auguste Bert)
Le Spectre de la Rose – M. Nijinsky
20.4 x 13.6 cm
(p.58)

Le Pavillon d'Armide – Madame Thamar Karsavina and M. Adolph Bolm
20.4 x 15.0 cm

Le Pavillon d'Armide – Madame Thamar Karsavina
20.4 x 15.2 cm

Le Carnaval – Monsieur Adolph Bolm
20.4 x 14.6 cm

Prince Igor – Madame Fedorova
20.4 x 15.4 cm

Prince Igor – Monsieur Adolph Bolm
20.4 x 15.2 cm
(p.7)

Cleopatra – Madame Fedorova
20.4 x 14.4 cm
(p.29)

(Auguste Bert)
Scheherazade – M. Nijinsky
20.4 x 14.0 cm
(p.57)

Eileen MAYO
Great Britain 1906–New Zealand 1994
also worked in Australia 1953–1962
Serge Lifar as Boreas in Zéphire et Flore,
from *Serge Lifar* (London:
C. W. Beaumont, 1928)
lineblock
33.0 x 27.8 cm
edition 22/500
National Gallery of Australia Research Library, Canberra, Feint Collection
(p.64)

Valentin SEROV
Russia 1865–1911
Poster of Anna Pavlova in Les Sylphides
1909
colour lithograph
187.0 x 158.0 cm
St Petersburg State Museum of Theatre and Music

Count Jean de STRELECKI
Portrait of Serge Diaghilev c.1910
gelatin silver photograph
22.0 x 16.0cm
St Petersburg State Museum of Theatre and Music
(p.4)

UNKNOWN
Auditorium of the Maryinsky Theatre
c.1890s
gelatin silver photograph
18.7 x 28.5 cm
St Petersburg State Museum of Theatre and Music

UNKNOWN
Tamara Karsavina as the Ballerina in Petrouchka Paris 1911
gelatin silver photograph,
autographed by Karsavina
32.3 x 19.0 cm
St Petersburg State Museum of Theatre and Music
(p.37)

UNKNOWN
Vera Fokina and Michel Fokine in Carnaval
gelatin silver photograph
13.6 x 8.6 cm
National Gallery of Australia, Canberra

UNKNOWN
Diaghilev's Ballets Russes before their departure from Chicago 1916
gelatin silver photograph
25.5 x 20.0 cm
St Petersburg State Museum of Theatre and Music

UNKNOWN
Igor Stravinsky
gelatin silver photograph,
autographed by Stravinsky
7.7 x 10.4; 10.9 x 17.8 cm
National Gallery of Australia, Canberra

UNKNOWN
Irina Baronova as Zobeide in Schéhérazade
1936–40
gelatin silver photograph
22.0 x 16.4 cm
National Gallery of Australia, Canberra

UNKNOWN
Australia
Scene from Les Présages 1936–40
gelatin silver photograph
16.2 x 11.4 cm
National Gallery of Australia, Canberra

Scene from Schéhérazade 1936–40
gelatin silver photograph
21.8 x 16.4 cm
National Gallery of Australia, Canberra

THEATRE PROGRAMS AND JOURNALS

Les Ballets Russes Program Officiel édité par Comœdia Illustré, June 1910
cover: **Design for Shah Zeman in Schéhérazade,** after Bakst
32.1 x 25.0 cm
National Gallery of Australia, Canberra
(p.78)

Les Ballets Russes Program Officiel édité par Comœdia Illustré, 15 June 1910
Designs for Schéhérazade, after Bakst
32.1 x 25.0 cm
National Gallery of Australia, Canberra

Program Officiel / Comœdia Illustré, vol.4, no.16, 15 May 1912
Design for the Faun in L'Aprés midi d'un faune, after Bakst
31.8 x 24.7 cm
National Gallery of Australia, Canberra

Comœdia Illustré, 4th year, no.17, 1 June 1912
cover: **Queen Thamar and the Prince in Thamar**, costumes by Bakst
31.7 x 24.6 cm
National Gallery of Australia Research Library
(p.8)

Serge Diaghileff's Ballet Russe, Metropolitan Opera, New York 1916
Design for a Bacchante in Narcisse and an almée in Schéhérazade, after Bakst
31.6 x 23.4 cm
National Gallery of Australia, Canberra

Ballets Russes à L'Opéra, May–June 1920
Designs for Le Astuzie femminili, after Sert
31.4 x 24.2 cm
National Gallery of Australia, Canberra

La Danse, vol.11, no.3, December 1920
cover: **Design for the Chinese Conjurer in Parade,** after Picasso
32.0 x 24.7 cm
National Gallery of Australia, Canberra

XXI Saison des Ballets Russes de Serge Diaghilev, Paris 1928
cover: **Design for Ode**, after Tchelitchev
colour offset lithograph, pin-pricked by hand
31.8 x 24.5 cm
National Gallery of Australia, Canberra
(p.23)

XXIIe Saison des Ballets Russes de Serge Diaghilev 1929
cover: **Design for Le Bal,** after de Chirico
lineblock, watercolour stencil
32.0 x 24.5 cm
National Gallery of Australia, Canberra
(p.16)

Col. W. de Basil's Ballet Russe Australia– New Zealand 1939–40 1939
pages 28–29, autographed photographs of dancers
28.5 x 22.2 cm
National Gallery of Australia Research Library, Canberra

Checklist compiled by: Rebecca Bilous, Christine Dixon, Danielle Fearn, Sheena Jack, Roger Leong, Anne Moten, Diana Woollard
Exhibition design: Jos Jensen
Textile conservation: Debbie Ward, Sarah Clayton, Micheline Ford, Margaret Roberts, Charis Tyrrel

ACKNOWLEDGEMENTS

From Russia with Love is the result of many people's work. Unfortunately, limited space prevents naming every contributor. Thanks are gratefully extended for their many good ideas.

Alan R. Dodge, Director, Art Gallery of Western Australia, and Natalia Metelitsa, Deputy Director, St Petersburg State Museum of Theatre and Music, have been instrumental to the project. This book has been greatly enriched by the insights of the authors: Lynn Garafola, Natalia Metelitsa, Michelle Potter, Nancy Van Norman Baer and Sarah Woodcock. It is with much regret that we note the recent death of Nancy Van Norman Baer, Curator, Theater and Dance at the Fine Arts Museums of San Francisco. She was a pioneer in the history of art, dance and theatre, and will be remembered for her knowledge and passion. Her contribution to this project was invaluable.

At the lending institutions, the assistance and support of staff has been critical; The Australian Ballet, Melbourne (Yvonne Gates, Ian McCrae, Colin Peasley); A.A. Bakhrushin State Central Theatre Museum, Moscow (Tatiana Klim); Comité André Masson, Paris (Guite Masson); Musée national d'art moderne—Centre de création industrielle, Paris (Didier Schulmann); National Film and Sound Archive, Canberra; Österreichisches Theatermuseum, Vienna (Peter Nics); St Petersburg State Museum of Theatre and Music (Irina Evstigneeva and staff); Theatre Museum, London (Margaret Benton, Sarah Woodcock); and the Victoria and Albert Museum, London (Susan Lambert, Janet Skidmore).

Support has come from Jean de Bestegui and the Bibliothèque nationale de France, Paris (Pierre Vidal); the Dansmuseet, Stockholm (Erik Näslund); Los Angeles County Museum of Art (Dale C. Gluckman); the Performing Arts Museum, Melbourne (Janine Barrand and staff); Serge Amburger; Ausdance, Canberra (Julie Dyson); Colleen and Michael Chesterman; Philip Dyer; Ted Gott; Robyn Healy; Wendy Jensen; Lindie Ward; Jill White; and the former de Basil dancers, Anna Volkova, Betty Tweddle and Valrene Tweedie. Michelle Potter's generous advice is greatly appreciated.

This project has been built on the collaboration, hard work and professionalism of all our colleagues at the National Gallery of Australia. Sincere thanks go to the Director, Brian Kennedy, for his enthusiastic support, and to Betty Churcher, our former Director. Special mention must also go to staff in the following departments: Conservation, especially the Textile Conservation section, Education and Public Programs, Exhibitions, International Art, Marketing and Publications, Photographic Services, Registration, Research Library, Travel, Workshop and Electricians.

To the talented people who volunteered their time and good will: above all, our former curator of Theatre Arts, Diana Woollard; Rebecca Bilous; Danielle Fearn; Claudia Hyles; Maria Inglis; Anne Moten; Voyka Savic; Pamela Tonkin; and Petronella Wensing. Lastly, to our families and friends for tolerating the absences.

Roger Leong and Christine Dixon
Curators
November 1998